S0-EFO-577

ABOVE ALL ELSE

ABOVE ALL ELSE

JUNE HUNT

Fleming H. Revell Company

Old Tappan, New Jersey

Unless otherwise identified, all Scripture quotations are from the King James Version of the Bible.

Scripture quotations identified NAS are from the New American Standard Bible, Copyright © THE LOCKMAN FOUNDATION 1960, 1962, 1963, 1968, 1971. Used by permission of The Lockman Foundation.

Scripture quotations identified LB are from The Living Bible, Copyright © 1971 by Tyndale House Publishers, Wheaton, Illinois 60187. All rights reserved.

Scripture quotations identified RSV are from the Revised Standard Version of the Bible, copyrighted 1946, 1952, © 1971 and 1973 by the Division of Christian Education of the National Council of Churches, and are used by permission.

Scripture quotations identified PHILLIPS are from THE NEW TESTAMENT IN MODERN ENGLISH, translated by J. B. Phillips. © J. B. Phillips 1958, 1960, 1972. Used by permission of Macmillan Publishing Co., Inc.

Scripture quotations identified AMPLIFIED are from the Amplified New Testament © The Lockman Foundation 1958, and are used by permission.

The song "Lonely Voices" by Billy Hanks, Jr., copyright © 1967 by the Hope Publishing Company, is used by permission.

REACH OUT AND TOUCH by Charles F. Brown, © Copyright 1971 by Word, Inc. All Rights Reserved. Used by permission.

WOULD YOU by Grace Hawthorne and Buryl Red, © Copyright 1972 by Word Music, Inc. All Rights Reserved. Used by permission.

Library of Congress Cataloging in Publication Data

Hunt, June.
　　Above all else.

　　1.　Christian life—1960–　　2.—Hunt, June.
I.　Title.
BV4501.2.H826　　248'.4　　74–13243
ISBN 0–8007–0689–7

Copyright © 1975 by June Hunt
Published by Fleming H. Revell Company
All Rights Reserved
Printed in the United States of America

TO *my father,*
from whom I gained many insights
which I didn't realize
I was learning
at the time

Contents

	Foreword	9
	Preface	11
	Introduction	15
1	Motives—We, the Glory-Seekers	19
2	Prayer—A Two-Way Street	27
3	Humility—Just Plain Folks	37
4	Listening—Watt's That You Said?	45
5	Sensitivity—Jogging, Jingles, and Jesus	53
6	Methods—Right or Wrong	59
7	God's Timing—Watch Out!	65
8	Freedom—And the Lack of It	71
9	Adversity—Joy Is Not an Electric Blanket	76
10	Message Music—Reach Out and Touch	81
11	Witnessing—In My Little Corner of the World	89
12	Meditation—To Succeed or Not to Succeed	98
13	Our Father—Hallowed or Hollow Be Thy Name	106
14	Temptation—A Familiar Face	112
15	Forgiveness—To the Very End	117
16	Decision—With Gratitude	124

Foreword

It was the great Christian ascetic and writer Thomas à Kempis who said, "Occasions do not make a man either strong or weak, but they show what he is."

So it is then, that when an affluent young lady chooses to describe materialism in terms of the Christian faith, her circumstances of affluence only show more clearly her true, noble, and godly character.

In this book June Hunt provides a fresh and provocative analysis of what belief in Christ really means. In a delightful style, she puts common problems in perspective. Her theme is letting God be God in our lives, and she develops it in a way that should make the reader anxious to try her suggestions.

Every page affords proof that God is *knowable*. She is committed to the thesis that God wants to be involved in our daily experiences—not as a judge so much as a helping friend.

With graphic language, June puts handles on contemporary imponderables. The reader identifies easily with every slice of life she depicts. With appropriate and delightful humor, she delves into the back rooms of daily living, and opens them to the healing and exuberance of the committed life.

This is a volume of insights. It is not penned by some aged, insulated ecclesiastic, but by a sensitive person, identified with young people by virtue of both church vocation and educational training. The distinction she draws separates the theoretical from the practical and the imagined from the real.

People involved even remotely with young people will want to read *Above All Else,* for the simple reason that it is replete with program specifics that really work.

No verbal overkill here; for in few and succinct terms, June Hunt has spelled out the formula for a Christian life that offers spiritual success and personal joy.

BILLY GRAHAM

Preface

I'd like to share a discovery with you.

God is not mainly a convenient *depressurizing* word to be used while releasing anger or frustration. He has not set up permanent residence behind ornate stained-glass windows. He has not folded His arms and positioned Himself on the soft cushions in the rear pews of our churches to observe our feeble talents.

What is God? Who is God? He is not only the Creator of everything positive that was, is, and will be, but He is also the Spirit who desires:

to give us strength to overpower our hidden weaknesses.
to give us wisdom when all we have is knowledge.
to give us sensitivity to people with whom we are insensitive.
to give us uncanny peace when confusion seems to reign.
to give us a caring heart to reach out to the unlovely.
to give us limitless love to touch those we *cannot* seem to love.

God's specialty is turning defeat into victory—in *His* way, in *His* time. If a person turns his life over to God completely, He will turn his uncharted wanderings into a plan with a purpose.

My personal struggle comes in letting *God be God in my life.* I wish I could say, "It's easy." For me it's not. Many times I've had to learn the hard way.

In this book I have shared experiences which I have had—my

personal encounters with man *and* God. A great joy will be to learn that you or a friend of yours has had a happier life adventure because of this book. You will have enabled me to serve God more completely. My failures will have become victories. My joys and successes will be enriched.

The following pages contain some truths which I have learned and am still learning from the *living* God who continues to teach me—slow learner though I may be.

JUNE HUNT

Acknowledgments

When it comes to expressing genuine gratitude to the friends who have been a part of the writing of this book, somehow my words seem much too empty. But to those who were willing to wade through the book with me, they must know my deepest appreciation. A few, however, I must mention by name:

Helen—my sister and my friend;

Mary Nance Rae—who at one call was willing to drop everything to give me the help I needed;

Sandy Lloyd and Barbara Spruill—who knew how to love and encourage me beyond words;

Lea Scott and Betty McAfee—who cheerfully typed, and retyped, and retyped, and retyped from my microscopic handwriting;

Joyce Norman—who gave me all the time and energy that she could possibly have given in editing this book;

Frances Duron, Betty Rogers—who were still proofing as the presses began to roll;

And last, but certainly not least:
my mother—who prayed me through it.

Introduction

As soon as I had unlocked the door and closed it behind me, I fell across the bed. For the first time in weeks I was absolutely alone—and face-to-face with the fascinating way in which God was working in my life.

Basically, I am a person who likes having people around. I thoroughly enjoy the interchange of ideas and the sharing of life. But not this night! I was happy to have only one companion with me—my overactive mind that began a replay of past events.

I thought back to the time when I resigned my job as college and career director at a large church in Dallas in order to accept previously received invitations to sing and speak. I had walked into the future not knowing where or to whom my new work would lead me.

While employed at the church, I had accepted invitations to perform or speak elsewhere and had always found these experiences to be great challenges. But when the doors seemed to be opening wide and the invitations were more numerous than I could accept, I was faced with the necessity of making a change.

So here I was, a thousand miles from home. A few hours earlier, I had spoken at a Christian Women's Club luncheon just sharing what I had come to learn about the Man, Jesus Christ. And, the night before, I had spoken on a college campus at a student rally. For months I had met engagements constantly, and every day for the past week I had spoken to groups whose evident hunger for the Christian message had overwhelmed me.

In addition to speaking and singing, my time had been filled with interviews, radio and TV appearances, appointments for personal counseling, and rap sessions on high-school and college campuses. I had been surrounded by people day and night and loved every bit of it.

During the three performances I gave the day before, something happened that made me smile. I had given the same basic program morning, noon, and evening; however, at the first program, twenty-one people opened their hearts to Christ; then, at the second appearance, seven made decisions. But, at the last appearance, one hundred fourteen responded. I couldn't help but wonder why the same number didn't respond at each place.

How clearly it came to me that God, and *only* God, touches people's hearts! I am available only for Him to use me. It is just a matter of letting God *be* God in my life.

But now I was thankful to be alone, able to absorb the welcome quiet. As my body and spirit responded to this soothing interlude, I found myself in absolute awe of the way God had worked.

I used to think that I went to church to serve God. I couldn't have been more wrong. We go to church so that God can serve us—for there are needs in our lives which only God can meet. In a similar way, as I speak and sing about Jesus Christ, I am not serving *Him. He* is serving *me.*

Within me is a potential which needs to be realized—a life message which must be expressed. Because I am created by God, it is He who knows how best to fulfill me. Even now, each time I see someone respond to the life Jesus Christ offers, I feel an exuberant joy. His *methods* may change, but His *message* remains the same.

In the past few years He has become so real to me that the necessity of telling this to others has been like a force propelling me forward day after day. The spiritual principles I have learned from life have made a great difference in my relationship to God and to my world. There is no greater satisfaction than that of being fulfilled by God.

I remember when the word *satisfaction* had another meaning for me. It might describe my feelings after tasting a slice of delicious German chocolate cake. Suppose a person bakes the cake but doesn't give me the recipe. I can see the cake, smell it, and touch it, but I cannot reproduce it. I cannot duplicate what gave me satisfaction unless the recipe is shared with me.

My purpose here is to share my recipe for Christian living in the hope that, if your recipe is incomplete, through some of my experiences and God's help, your own life will find completeness.

You will see here the word *recipe.* When you do, know that for a complete life—filled with God's presence—the *recipe* is God's instruction to each of us. It takes *all* of the ingredients to achieve the oneness with Christ we all desire.

My theme is that of letting God *be* God in our lives as I share experiences I have had where I witnessed God *being* God.

No one Bible verse stands apart as my favorite; however, many are extremely personal and meaningful to me. God's Word is alive and He desires to give us all new life if we will partake of the Scriptures.

As I examine my own life, I realize that the depth of my life and message hinges on my motives. This awareness drives me to find a Scripture with which to test my motives, and I discover in the Book of Psalms, "Search me, O God, and know my heart; test my thoughts. Point out anything you find in me that makes you sad . . ." (139:23 LB). I have found that many times God indeed is pointing—only I'm not looking.

The Christian life is one of discoveries and every day reveals one—or two—or eight new ones. God is *knowable*—and that discovery can be the beginning for you.

1

Motives—We, the Glory-Seekers

We can justify our every deed but God looks at our motives.

Proverbs 21:2 LB

There are times when we read the Bible seeking comfort and solace and we find the comfortable words. More often, I find direction for making changes which will carry me forward in my Christian life. I can justify every deed as the Scripture verse indicates, but if God is looking at my motives I had better examine them, too. This puts the pressure on me to follow God's Word —I am compelled to change as the Scriptures lead me to become the person God has promised that I can become, and that I want to be.

How well I remember the first painful pressure I really felt! It was during my freshman year at Southern Methodist University. I had eaten an early dinner and when I returned to the dorm I found a close friend lying across her bed. She had attempted suicide with an overdose of sleeping pills. How strange she looked to me—the response was that of a limp doll as I attempted to arouse her.

Stunned, I ran back to the cafeteria and got my brother whom I had seen eating there earlier and together we carried my friend to the university's health clinic.

Later that evening in the quiet of my room, I thought about

her absence. Only hours before I had referred to her as a friend, but now she seemed like a stranger to me. Of all the people I knew, this girl was the last person I would have expected to attempt suicide. She was a very personable and sincere girl, projecting the image of the always-happy type.

Coming back to the dorm after one of my brief visits with my friend in the clinic, I stopped at our joint mailbox. Inside was the bill for her medical treatment. I suddenly did something that is extremely unusual for me—something I had never done before. I opened the bill, took it inside and wrote out a check to cover the full amount. Somehow, it seemed important to me that she not find out who had paid the bill.

Normally, I would have taken great pride in being so giving; yet now, I was taking every precaution to prevent her from knowing. A staggering thought hit me: *How many gifts would I have given if the recipients had never known the gifts came from me?*

I made myself examine my motives for giving, and I finally realized there should be no motivation for giving other than the happiness of the recipient—*with God getting the glory.* I find it extremely difficult to measure myself with the Scripture, "Whatsoever ye do, do all to the glory of God" (1 Corinthians 10:31). I fear that too often the gift-givers are the glory-seekers.

As I came face-to-face with this verse, I wondered what would happen if I, June Hunt, did everything for God's glory alone. *Every* motivation originating from Him! In that moment, I knew with certainty that I must stop endlessly comparing myself with others and keep my eyes on Christ.

That's a tall order! *Everything* for the glory of God? Is it probable? Well, maybe not probable, but most certainly possible.

"To the glory of God" is not just another phrase we're supposed to tack onto the end of a prayer full of Lord-I-need phrases. "To the glory of God" is the expression of our purpose for every day in our lives. There should be no other motivation for anything we do. No compromise! In his book, *A Spiritual Clinic,* Oswald J. Sanders offers to the reader a measuring rod for motives: "Is its supreme objective the glory of God and not the glory of the disciple? Will its fulfillment make the disciple more useful in Christ's service and a greater blessing to his fellow men?"

We weren't put on this earth to please mankind, but we are free to choose the focus of our struggle for acceptance. Should we look to God or to man for acceptance?

If we look to man, inevitably we compare ourselves with others. The damaging results of using people as standards of comparison boil down to two basic things: inferiority and superiority. God never suggested we draw comparisons with each other. The only Person with whom God intends us to compare ourselves is Jesus Christ. So, after an honest look at my motives, I began to see that I was seeking acceptance from man. When we become fully aware that God accepts us, we need not worry about *man's* opinion of us. We no longer have to struggle with motives. Instead, the driving force within us is one of love, and we reflect the presence of our Lord.

This concept was reinforced during the time I was a youth director at the First Baptist Church of Dallas. I knew that a fourteen-year-old boy (whom I'll call Dave Todd) had been spilling tacks down the ramps of the parking garage. I really liked Dave, "all boy" that he was.

Quickly, I located Mrs. Todd, who was nearby with a friend, and informed her of what I knew regarding her son. The friend quietly slipped into another room as I subsequently revealed four other things Dave had done. I operated under the premise that if I were a parent, I would want to know if there were any question regarding my child's behavior.

That evening I received a phone call from Dr. Todd, a powerful, highly influential doctor: "Meet me at your office tomorrow!" he said. "And you had better be ready to make your statements stand up in court."

I was petrified! The thought of this confrontation put me in a state of panic. Mechanically, I replaced the receiver on the hook. Then came the obvious question we all *should* ask in times of stress: Did I do anything to cause even *a part* of this problem? The question is crucial—so is the answer.

First of all, I committed an inexcusable error by confronting Mrs. Todd in the presence of a third party. I was so wrapped up in what *I* had to say that I appeared totally insensitive to *both* women. I failed to use my "praise in public—confront in private" philosophy.

In addition, I realized my initial, matter-of-fact approach had been wrong. One could say a confrontation should be put together like a sandwich: the meat of the meeting (the criticism) sandwiched between two cushions of bread (praise and exhortation).

> Bread is *praise* which reinforces self-worth.
> Meat is *criticism* which evaluates the problem and includes a solution.
> Bread is *exhortation* which motivates the person to action.

Praising the strong points and qualities of a person prevents potential barriers from being raised; therefore, objectivity is possible and the person involved can actually become excited about the working out of possible solutions.

The *way* in which I approached Mrs. Todd could and should have been with much more empathy. Mrs. Todd was alarmed by the manner in which I informed her.

The following morning after a restless night, I went to the conference room before it was time for the confrontation. I asked a man who had knowledge of some of the boy's other offenses to meet with us. Both Dr. and Mrs. Todd appeared promptly at 9 A.M.

At the beginning of the conference I asked Mrs. Todd if she would forgive me for being insensitive to her as a mother. She did. However, any momentary relief which I might have felt from her response was overshadowed by the contrast of Dr. Todd's attitude.

Concerning the meeting, which lasted almost three hours, I can truthfully say that up to this point in my life I had never been talked to in such a manner. Dr. Todd would ask a question, and then when I began my answer, he would cut me off in mid-sentence with sarcastic antagonism. Over and over again he cut me off. It made no difference that I had something to say. He wasn't listening.

Amid the heated intensity of Dr. Todd's mock trial, complete with accusations and veiled threats, I chose to say nothing. Dr. Todd continued his attack which became a loud monotone in the background of my mind as I began to talk to God. "Lord, I know You're letting this continue to teach me something and I do want to learn what it is." I prayed this way because I realized that God does not make mistakes. *It is more than important that we know this.* It is essential. GOD DOES NOT MAKE MISTAKES. To those who have committed their lives to Him nothing happens by accident. Therefore, I knew God had me in this situation for a purpose.

My natural response would have been to fight back verbally, but I realized loss of composure and a defensive attitude would accomplish nothing, so I managed to maintain a calmness that really surprised me.

I twice interjected, "Pardon me, sir, but can we pray about this?" Each time the response was negative.

While I saw that I was getting nowhere, I did realize that my perspective regarding the total situation was limited, but not so with God. God doesn't see merely the stone tossed into the water; He sees both the splash and the ripples caused by the stone.

I am convinced that if our *response* is right, the *result* will be right. God even goes so far as to assure, "When a man's ways please the Lord, he maketh even his enemies to be at peace with him" (Proverbs 16:7).

Although the father attacked my character and threatened my job, I had no bitterness for this man. Shaken up, yes. Bitter, no. God taught me one of the most valuable lessons I could ever hope to learn: We are not responsible for our reputations when we are totally committed to God and His purposes. Our reputation is God's responsibility. Our responsibility is to see that our motives reflect the will of God.

Three days after the conference at the church, Dave was caught letting air out of tires in the parking garage. Even though I was immediately told about this incident, I let another person handle the notification of the parents. You see, I knew how easy it would have been for me to have the I told-you-so attitude.

God always writes the last chapter. In fact, months later God was still writing. On a Sunday evening I spotted Dave waiting for me near a side door at the church. I approached not knowing what to expect from him. He had little to say in words, but said much with a single tear and a boyishly awkward hug.

The imperfection in Christians enables those who don't know Christ to attack the Christian church and thus try to substantiate their belief that the church is full of hypocrites. One man came right out and told me, "That's why I don't go to church. Everybody there is a hypocrite."

I have no problem when people say there are hypocrites in the church. Sure there are! I'd be the first to agree; but then, there are hypocrites in life. Businesses are full of them. There is not one of us who has not at some time represented himself as being better than he is—a hypocrite; but for some reason the church catches the credit for having *all* the hypocrites.

Yet, that's the purpose of the church—to minister to all of us who *are* imperfect, and to minister to the hypocritical part in each of us.

A singer named Deni not long ago asked Christ into her life. Her honest statement was, "Jesus Christ was the first Christian I met whom I really liked."

We are all imperfect. We are all very human. Only one was flawless—Jesus Christ. Make no mistake: Jesus Christ intends to minister to our weaknesses—*if we will let Him.* If our motives are within His will, He can refine and make usable those things about us that we may recognize as undesirable.

Wallace Henley, journalist and author, states that because many of us consider some of our motives undesirable, we become bogged down in motive mud piles:

"We know we are full of imperfections," Henley said. "Does this mean, then, that we don't worry about pure motives anymore? That neat cop-out is not available to the Christian. We must affirm that our motives are mixtures of pure *and* impure drives. We don't stop acting on these motives just because they have impure elements, any more than we take up residence in an isolated cave because there is some sin out there in the world.

"But this the Christian does: He acts, recognizing the ambivalence of his motives, all the while trying to press toward that pure motive that is his goal."

This concept is beautifully illustrated through the experience of a friend in California. Her husband felt no need for Christ or the church in his life, and to make matters worse, communication was a foreign word to the family. Based on the Scripture, "Wives, submit yourselves unto your own husbands" (Ephesians 5:22), she and her children agreed on a project which they called "The King Is Coming."

Each evening when the husband came home from work, he found the children neat, his wife attractively dressed, the house spotless, and a warm dinner on the table. In every instance, the man was treated like royalty. At first he thought, "This won't last long," but after six weeks of this consistent attention, some real changes occurred. Communication and love transcended to a higher level than they thought possible.

The wife realized that many of the things she had done for him previously had been done with no thought for him *personally*. She was really seeking his praise. Not realizing it, she had been motivated by her desire for self-glory. But now she looked at him in a new light—from God's point of view, that is, loving him without reservation. And as a result her new motive was only that of meeting his needs.

When Jesus looks at a person, He doesn't see merely the exterior, but rather the interior—the full potential of the heart and the entire life. What this wife had not done was look for that interior. In fact, she looked for no potential at all. But things changed when *she* changed.

By showing God's love, a mother and her children helped a man know the King is coming—again!

2

Prayer—A Two-Way Street

I had been involved in a student organization at SMU for three years when a new member, to whom I found it difficult to relate, was put in a position over me. Because our relationship was not what I felt it should be, I went to him in an attempt to build better lines of communication. However, nothing changed.

In reflecting on the situation now, I think he felt inadequacies, because I was more experienced than he; and *I* felt resentment because he got much credit for work that I did. I can recall times when his face would end up in a "mud puddle" and I would say, "Let me help you," adding inwardly, ". . . drown."

Then one afternoon I did some serious thinking about it and said to myself, "June, this isn't right. As a Christian your attitude is all wrong toward this guy." After praying for God to change him, I began to read in the Book of Proverbs.

Suddenly it was as if a Sherman tank had run over me, leaving deep track marks, for I read: "Do not rejoice when your enemy meets trouble. Let there be no gladness when he falls . . ." (24:17 LB). Well, he wasn't exactly an enemy, but neither were we friends. Then driving the track marks even deeper was, "Pray for your enemies."

I started thinking about the word *pray* and it dawned on me that I had not been praying *for him.* I had been praying, "Lord, change this situation so *I* can feel better about it," thus benefitting *me.* My motive had been basically selfish, for I never had

27

genuinely stopped to consider his needs and pray on his behalf. This was drastically wrong. No wonder I wasn't getting results!

When I began praying intently *for* him our relationship improved. I now realize it was my attitude that needed to be changed, for I discovered that you cannot pray sincerely for someone else and remain detached. *You cannot pray consistently for someone without feeling a loving concern for him.*

When a woman in Indiana told me that her marriage was in difficulty, she admitted communication lines were broken between her and her husband. I asked this very fine Christian woman who knew much about the Bible if she had prayed genuinely for her husband. She hesitated. I asked her again, "Have you prayed not thinking of yourself at all, but thinking solely about *him?* Like 'Lord, teach my husband how to become wise and make him a man of compassion and strength. Let this be done for *his* sake alone. I pray out of honest concern for him.' "

Her eyes became bright and she said, "Why, I've never thought about it that way. I see now that I've been praying selfish prayers. When I do things for him at home, it's really so he will praise me. It's true, my motives are not right."

In all fairness to this woman, I must point out that she doesn't stand alone in praying erroneously. At times we all do. Even the followers of Jesus were guilty of this. It is recorded in Acts 12 that a group had gathered at the home of Mary, mother of John Mark, to pray for the release of imprisoned Peter. They were greatly concerned because King Herod was planning to have Peter, their leader, executed after Passover. To Herod, Peter's death meant he would just be free of another fanatic, so a large group was praying.

When they heard a knock at Mary's gate, Rhoda went to the door. She recognized Peter's voice and became so excited she forgot to open the door. Instead, she rushed inside to tell those praying, "Peter is outside!" They didn't believe her, they just couldn't! Meanwhile, there stood Peter, knocking away, while the group inside was exclaiming to Rhoda, "You're out of your mind!" None of them understood the power of God and the reality of answered prayer.

Out on the street stood the *answer* to their prayers—still knocking at the door! Finally, they went to see for themselves. There was Peter. What a picture! Here this group was indeed praying—but with *no faith!* At the first knock, every man of them should have leaped to his feet and exclaimed with assurance, "That must be Peter." They had been praying for his release, hadn't they?

In the first chapter of James we are told to pray without doubting. But where was this group's faith? (It must have been in prison with Peter, for apparently he was the only one who had any at all.) Pray *believing*. That's the key. Even today our faith is often in prison, bound only by our lack of willingness to believe.

Too many of us pray with a negative attitude, and by our negativism we try to second-guess God. When a teen-ager approaches his mother with, "I don't suppose I can go to the movies tonight?" he's asking, but his question has the overtone of an already answered statement. There is doubt in his mind, and he is expressing it by the manner in which he asks the question.

We may not phrase our petitions to God in just that exact way, but we might as well, for we ask many times fully expecting the answer to be negative. We are told to ask *believing*, and that's positive! We must all learn to pray with expectancy and faith. Pray believing and trust Him for the answer. It's not that we depend on our prayers, but through prayer we depend on God.

In my early years as a supposed Christian, the only way I really talked to God was in what I call "panic prayers." I'd get in a tight spot and start the dear-God-help-me . . . help-me . . . help-me . . . routine. I had the attitude that God was my little helper, just waiting around in case of emergencies.

Occasionally, I uttered stale words that probably got no farther than my ceiling, but nothing came from my heart. That's understandable. How can a prayer come from the heart when the heart is empty? It doesn't matter what one prays for or how eloquently he expresses himself. What does matter is that God *must* live within. When Christ is in the heart, He gives *power* to prayer.

At times we may wonder why our prayers don't seem powerful. It could be because we've never asked the Source of Power into our lives; or, it could be because we pray incorrectly.

For example, should we desire more patience, we don't pray, "God, *help* me to have more patience." *God is not our little helper!* He *is* patience, and *if* He is living inside us, we don't need any *more* of anything. You see, we have it all. Acknowledge that He *is* the Source who enables us to develop our full potential. Paul emphasizes that, "Not in your own strength for it is God who is all the while effectually at work in you—energizing and creating in you the power and desire. . . ." (*See* Philippians 2:13 AMPLIFIED.)

Therefore, on our own, we can obtain no more patience, tolerance, or anything else. The self has simply got to die and God's Spirit must have full control in our lives—not as an assistant or helper, but as Lord! It is a matter of letting God *be* patience, *be* tolerance, *be* understanding, and *be* love through us. He is there and He is all these things we pray for so many times, and the answer is just to let go and let God *be* God in our lives.

Not only must we recognize "Christ within," we must also accept the way in which He chooses to work in our lives. Simply put, when we pray, we should accept the way He answers even if it seems illogical, as in the story of a man who was standing on the edge of a mountain viewing the scenery. Excited over the view, he got too close to the edge and fell over. As he was going down, he grabbed a limb protruding from the side of the mountain and began yelling, "Somebody help me! God? You there? I need help!"

A voice spoke loud and clear, "I'm here. Now, listen to me. What you must do is let go of the limb."

The little man, with his feet dangling in midair, called back, "Uh, is there somebody else there I could talk to?"

It's this business of faith—total faith in our God who makes no mistakes.

In addition to having faith we also need to understand the difference between *saying* a prayer and *praying* a prayer. This distinction between the two was brought home to me through an experience I had as a teen-ager in our church choir. After each practice, different members closed with prayer. I escaped being asked to pray aloud by always looking down or bending over to get my purse. Every Sunday at 5:30 P.M. I turned into a female version of the Hunchback of Notre Dame.

I had no idea what it was like to talk to God aloud, not having done so in the church I had previously attended. I didn't know you just *talked* to Him like you would to a friend. Prayer is not a monolog: it is a dialog. Prayers are answered by God and He intends for us to hear His answers.

One day, however, I was called upon to dismiss the choir with prayer. Panic struck! I just hoped to get out some pretty good sentences that would sound kind of religious. In the middle of my prayer I got stuck. I simply couldn't think of anything more to say and I completely forgot how to end a prayer. Finally, after a long pause, I remembered, "Amen." I learned there is a vast difference between *saying* prayers and *praying.*

Although eventually I was on a large church staff, one thing about praying continued to puzzle me. I had heard about people praying for hours—and some all night long! How could that be? What could they possibly say?

Projects are always a challenge so I decided to try one on prayer. I determined that after I got into my car each morning, I would pray the entire time until I reached my office. That very day I started my experiment at the beginning of my twenty-minute trip. After a few minutes I noticed a woman walking her dog and I started thinking about my parents' two dogs. When I arrived at the parking garage I realized my prayers had been interrupted and my thought processes had traveled throughout the entire animal kingdom! But I wasn't about to give up.

The next day I knew I had to pray aloud in order to stay on track. I began again, but once I got through my "list"—family, co-workers, and a few friends—I got stuck again. I said, "Now,

Lord, I really don't know what to say so You'll just have to tell me what to pray for. I'll just keep on talking."

I remember thinking about several people for whom I had never prayed, one being Sally Baker. As things about her job began to come to mind, I prayed for her all the way to the office. (To be honest, when I *finally* arrived at the parking garage, it was the most gorgeous building I'd ever seen.)

Normally, when I entered the youth area, Sally would be facing me and I would call, "Hi, Sally," as I turned into my office. This particular day I gave my good-morning greeting while wheeling toward my door, but I kept turning until I had completed a three-hundred-sixty degree circle. I walked over to Sally's desk, sat down, and started talking with her. For the first time I realized she was more than just a secretary sitting behind a desk. I was seeing her as a person of worth and purpose.

To those who have never experienced such a thing, this may sound strange, but I actually saw a transformation take place in a matter of days. Sally could sense my new attitude, and began immediately to respond. She seemed to have a new interest in me and my work, and I could tell that her job became more than just a job. Our relationship took on new meaning with a unity and oneness of mind, and as a result, our work became more enjoyable. I had almost walked past a friendship which was to become very meaningful in my life.

God gave me a new sensitivity and awareness about people as I *committed* myself to a regular time of prayer. God says, "Pray without ceasing," so obviously He considers prayer *essential*—not merely desirable. God will bring situations to our minds for which we need to pray if we simply commit ourselves to talking with Him and put no time limit on the conversation. Somehow I can't envision God holding a stopwatch over us.

At the beginning of my five years on the staff of Dallas's eighteen-thousand member First Baptist Church, I had to learn how to work with the junior-high adult leadership, which involved one hundred twenty individual personalities.

After three years of working (or rather surviving), I was engaged in conversation with one of my leaders, Edith Hardison. She confided that when I first became junior-high director she realized only God could teach me the many things I needed to know. She added, "So, another person and I decided we would pray regularly that God would teach you as fast as possible and equip you to handle this mammoth job."

Well, this really came as a surprise! I had no idea Edith was praying for me, but when I found she had been doing so consistently for three years, my sense of awareness and appreciation for her changed—changed to the point that after that evening I always looked for Edith when I walked into a room of workers. If she were sitting in a meeting I was conducting, I felt her presence not only encouraged me, but also gave me added confidence. To be truthful, I'd feel like Popeye after having downed a can of spinach!

You see, when a person is challenged, he will travel on one of two avenues—that of success or that of failure. She had challenged me, but the power of prayer had erased any *fear* of failure. Overnight she had changed from worker to friend and through this personal encounter I made a discovery: *When you find someone is praying for you in a loving way, you cannot help but respond to that individual.*

As a result of this discovery, I decided to plan a project with a group of college and career young people who met weekly. "Get with another person you don't know well," I requested. "Now, I want you to share one problem or difficulty about which your partner can pray for one week. And I mean pray *every single day.*"

A week later we all met again, and without exception each looked forward with some anticipation to seeing his partner. Before the meeting, Grace Dowell asked if she could say something to the group. "Because of a bad situation, I'd wanted to change jobs," she began. "I asked my partner to pray for me because I didn't know what to do. Then at the end of the week I was offered another job with increased pay, free lunch, expenses, and a great boss. This *is* an answer to prayer!" Several others who were struggling with anger and bitterness reported improvement in attitudes. But what interested me the most was that the temperature of the group had become warmer and more personal. The response of these young people toward each other had changed and that surprised even them.

One fellow told the group, "I've never gone in for the prayer-partner bit before, but I thought I just might give it a try. Besides, it was only for a week. Since I've been meeting with you these past three months, I've been coming only out of habit. But man, I really did want to be here tonight to see how my partner was doing. I don't have anything special to say, but for the first time I somehow feel a part of the group."

He began to feel that he was a part because he had invested his time praying for someone else. And through this encounter I learned that *when you pray for someone else in a loving way, you cannot help but respond.*

One of the group's favorite projects was when everyone went off by himself to talk to God aloud. I instructed them to think of one thing they never thought of thanking God for, and then to talk to Him about it. I had done this myself before meeting with them and I had chosen electricity as my item. The purpose of this exercise was to *extend* their sense of awareness beyond those things which are routinely listed in prayers of gratitude. As strange as it may sound, my appreciation has been immeasurably increased for the many everyday things I would otherwise have taken for granted. God increases our sensitivity to those things for which we pray—even electricity.

I gave the same instruction to a large group of adults. The following day a woman told me that the entire group had decided to do the project together; however, this time they thanked God for one *person* about whom they had never thought to be thankful. This same woman said there had been remarkable improvements in the attitudes of many members. In fact, the entire complexion of the group had changed so much that they were sensitive to the needs and desires of each other for the first time. I don't know why I continue to be amazed when I see that, *indeed,* prayer changes things. Attitudes, people, and *situations.* And it's through these situations—the ones where you sometimes feel totally hemmed in—that you can often see the greatest answer to prayer.

Such was the case one summer when a disastrous theft occurred. June McNamara and I were directors of a Christian camp for approximately six hundred young people. Two weeks prior to the opening of the camp, all of the registration cards and most of the money was stolen from June's car. Completely discouraged, we felt there was no way we could run the camp. It was impossible to get the registration cards redone on everyone in time to finish all of the work necessary to open camp. And then there was the matter of the money. Even if we could have replaced the cards and all the necessary information, a camp program of this size costs many thousands of dollars. Where would the money come from?

I assured June the problem was out of our hands. In other words, we gave the camp, the money, *and* the cards to God. The problem was out of *our* control. Only God could do something about this situation, and since the main purpose of the camp was to enrich the lives of the youth through a personal relationship with God, in reality the camp belonged to God. If He didn't want the camp to be held, we were honestly willing to accept it. I mean we really gave it *totally* to Him. All the months of preparation suddenly didn't matter. We gave His camp back to Him. Then we told God if there was some creative alternative we had not thought of, we'd be open to it. June and I both walked away from that time of prayer with complete confidence in the *Lord's* ability.

Great was our reward! Several hours later, June received word that the police had found some of the stolen articles strewn along a service road by a Dallas lake. Although there were tire marks over a number of the cards, not one was destroyed, nor blown into

the lake, nor missing. As incredible as it may sound, we were able
to account for every cent of the money!

I have experienced projects which work and I've seen prayers
answered beyond coincidence and human comprehension, but I
still have much to learn about the power of prayer. I can remember many times I thought God had not answered my prayers. I
often forgot that _no_ and _wait_ are also answers. Fortunately, God
knows the deepest desires of our hearts and He knows how and
when to give us those desires. Make no mistake: *God's timing is
perfect.* He also realizes that there are times when, if He were to
give us everything for which we ask, He would not be helping us
fulfill those desires. God's noes are just as much expressions of His
love as his yeses.

From my childhood, mother taught me to trust God's noes
because we are often blinded by our immediate need. A poem she
often shared with me expresses this concept beautifully.

> I asked for strength that I might achieve:
> He made me weak that I might obey.
> I asked for health that I might do greater things;
> I was given grace that I might do better things.
> I asked for riches that I might be happy;
> I was given poverty that I might be wise.
> I asked for power that I might have the praise of men;
> I was given weakness that I might feel the need of God.
> I asked for all things that I might enjoy life;
> I was given life that I might enjoy all things.
> I received nothing that I asked for, all that I hoped for.
> My prayer was answered.

ANONYMOUS

3
Humility—Just Plain Folks

A great influence in my life is the close relationship I share with my mother. Because of Dad's industries, Mom has often had the responsibility for entertaining visiting royalty, important diplomats, and well-known celebrities from all over the world; however, she has never been too busy for her children. Many nights Mom and I sit propped up on her bed talking, and our times spent like this are among my favorites. I love my mother for many reasons. Her sense of humor is beautiful and we laugh together a lot. She loves sharing life with me—all phases of it.

Her eyes dance at the thought of surprising someone—things like putting a gift under someone's plate at dinner. Mother has an insatiable desire to give of herself materially and spiritually.

But most of all I love my mother because she is a praying Christian! I count myself extremely fortunate to have a mother whose prayer life is a vital part of her existence. There is nothing vague about her conversations with God and she prays with much faith.

Mother is also the most humble person I know. She desires no credit for herself. In fact, she does all she can to avoid it by turning her attention to others. On Mother's Day, after the family gives their gifts to her, it is not unlike Mom to go to such great lengths expressing love and appreciation that the giver feels like the receiver. It is impossible to outgive Mother, especially where love is involved. Nor does this giving of herself stop with the family.

I remember the time when Mom arrived home hours late from an out-of-town trip. When she finally did get home, she related to us that a young soldier sat beside her on the plane, and through their conversation, she learned that a mix-up in flight scheduling would cause him to miss his family who planned to meet him. After Mom picked up her baggage she noticed the young man standing around in the waiting room with a dejected expression. On an impulse Mother insisted that she drive him the forty miles to his family's home. Mom literally beamed as she described the excitement the young soldier expressed as they neared his home and family.

I mention this incident only because it is so typical of Mom. There's a plaque in Mom's kitchen that really expresses her philosophy: BLOOM WHERE YOU ARE PLANTED.

I've also learned so much from the delicate way my parents handled their daily life together. Dad may have been a world-renowned industrialist and financier, but when he and Mom were at home together, it was hard to imagine him being anyplace else. On the front porch he loved to watch the "show" (his term for watching the moon and the stars). Some may find it difficult to imagine H. L. Hunt and his wife enjoying such simple pleasures, but frequently I found them simply sitting quietly on the porch holding hands. They had been together a long time and words were not always needed for conversation between them.

Even harder for some to believe is the fact that my father always delighted in singing for anyone with a listening ear—or otherwise! The favorite, and one they called *their* song, is "Just Plain Folks." In part it goes:

> We are just plain folks, your mother and me,
> Just plain folks like our own folks used to be . . .
> Yes, we're just—plain—folks.

I have heard this song many times in my lifetime, yet it never fails to affect me very deeply. That's my favorite time to imagine my dad—holding Mom's hand and singing, "We're Just Plain

Folks." Why? Because I realize that in Dad's quest to industrial-
ize, he had to forfeit things, one of them being a simple way of
life. Tears often came to his eyes because as he sang it, he believed
it.

My dad's appreciation for "plain folks" was always encouraged
by the fact that Mom never lost sight of the important values of
life. She schooled us in the basics so that our lives would be
founded on Christ rather than our immediate circumstances. I
realize now that Mom's beautiful humility was and is the result
of prayer. Prayer and humility walk hand in hand—the more one
prays, the more one grows in humility. Perhaps that is why the
struggle with pride is one of my biggest battlefields. I forget to
use God's artillery: prayer.

For example, should I decide to play the guitar in a concert,
I wouldn't think of beginning the performance with my guitar
untuned. How strange that I handle my life with far less concern,
for there are many times when I fail to get in tune with God at
the beginning of each day. Each time I stand to sing, I must
sincerely ask God to keep me aware that it is *His* performance.
I remember a period of time when, prior to singing, I cautiously
prayed, "Lord, please stop me if ever I attempt to sing on my own
power or for my own glory." One day He did.

I had been looking forward to singing for a special group.
While walking up to the stage, I remember thinking, "I'll really
impress them today!" After beginning my song with this definite
overconfidence, I approached the climaxing high note which I'd
accomplished hundreds of times before. Suddenly, my voice
cracked wider than the Grand Canyon. I was humiliated. Since
this had never happened to me before, I immediately thought of
my prayer. Isn't this exactly what I had asked the Lord to do—
to stop me if self-glory ever became a temptation? I had become
a living example of Proverbs: "Pride goes before destruction and
haughtiness before a fall" (16:18 LB).

One never graduates from the school of learning. God knew I
had much to learn about pride and humility, so He began teaching me early.

In the fall that I entered the ninth grade, my father decided to send my two sisters and me to a private school in Dallas, the Hockaday School for Girls. Truthfully, at the time I didn't really want to change schools, but I can now understand the meaning it had in my life. Although the school wasn't easy, my experiences there have proved to be invaluable. I found there were many advantages at a small girls' school. For instance, in a co-ed school boys are traditionally at the head of most organizations, but in a girls' school there is a noticeable shortage of boys! Therefore, each girl has a greater opportunity to realize her potential as an individual and as a possible leader. (To be honest, we would have rather had the boys.)

I was a very shy person and for the first two years didn't have any real friends. All I can really remember about those particular years is that people wrote things in my yearbook about my "nice smile." Things changed markedly by my senior year, and with God's help I acquired more self-confidence and a better understanding of myself. But a day was to come that would teach me even more.

Each year an honor was awarded at Hockaday called The Courtesy Cap. The entire student body voted for those students who were the most courteous and genuine. Afterward, the members of the faculty expressed their opinions by use of the blackball.

Also, during that same day the cast was to be announced for the spring musical *The Wizard of Oz*. Everyone just knew I would get the part of the Lion and all the kids kept congratulating me ahead of time. Anyway, I was president of the choir, so that sort of cinched it.

That morning I received a note requesting my presence at my advisor's office. After asking me to sit down she began: "Something has happened I know is going to hurt you." (I couldn't imagine what she could be talking about.) "You did not get a lead in the musical, June. I know everybody has been assuming you'd get the part of the Lion, but something unusual happened. I thought you ought to know this before the parts are announced so you can prepare yourself."

The casting went this way: the president of the student body got the Scarecrow; the president of the senior class got the Tin Man, and the girl best suited for the Dorothy role got Dorothy. However, two girls were being considered for Dorothy, so the other senior girl got the Lion role.

I was stunned. It had never even occurred to me that I wouldn't get one of the leads. An hour later, I was stunned again. The Courtesy Cap was awarded, and I didn't get that, either. It was just as with the musical—friends had been saying, "You'll get it," and I honestly thought I would, too.

What a humbling experience not to get *anything* at all, especially when everyone is expecting you to get *everything*. The most painful challenge came at the end of the choir period when I, as president, was asked to announce the names of those who had received leads in the musical. (I didn't even get the Witch!)

I felt I had no right to take away any excitement from the others by showing my deep disappointment; so, in one of the most intense prayers I've ever prayed, I asked for help: "Please God, take over my emotions so I can talk in a loving manner. I especially want to have no feelings in my heart against the director or the girl who got 'my' Lion part."

I would not be very human or truthful if I were to say I did not hurt. And since I didn't have any real close friends at the school I had to hold my disappointments inside. However, I consoled myself with the Scripture: "If you will humble yourselves under the mighty hand of God, in His good time He will lift you up" (*see* James 4:10).

Well, I'd been humbled and I realized God knew what His purpose was. I believed in the last part of the verse, too, and knew that He would ". . . lift me up." I'm not implying I said that verse and immediately the problems were solved. They weren't! But God's Word *always* helps.

I recall several girls saying, "You're actually smiling, June. What are you so happy about?" To be honest, if I hadn't smiled

I would have cried. A coach has said, "There are no good losers, there are just good actors. Everyone worth his salt desires to win!" I don't know about the salt, but I did want to win.

I remember after school that day, as soon as I stepped into my car the tears started to come. And they kept coming. My heart was broken. However, I also remember praying that God would give me the right attitude and teach me all I needed to learn through those experiences. Most important of all, I didn't want to be bitter in any way or let any negative attitude surface. But I was young, and human, and disappointed, and I only wished that a few people had had more faith in me.

Through that painful experience at Hockaday, I realized that humility often comes as the *result* of a painful lesson. And because of this awareness, I have always had great admiration for the truly humble person. There are those who would make the humble synonymous with a doormat weakling of Milquetoast character. Nothing can be further from the truth.

It takes a tremendous amount of strength to achieve humility. The humble person has won *freedom* from pride and arrogance, and achieved *victory* over conceit and condemnation. That's why God advises: "Clothe yourselves with humility toward one another, for God is opposed to the proud, but gives grace to the humble" (*see* James 4:6).

For me, if one person could personify humility, it would be John the Baptist. As Jesus' advance man, John—rugged, outspoken—was never to get top billing; and the beautiful thing is that *he knew it* and didn't mind!

He had a following of disciples and many believed John to be the promised Messiah, so it is easy to see his followers' jealousy and concern when they learned a man named Jesus was baptizing in the river Jordan, too.

They told John, ". . . everybody is going over there instead of coming here to us" (John 3:26 LB). They felt their ministry threatened and they were frightened.

John calmly and without any fanfare told them his function was to prepare people so they would go to Him. And he added, "I am filled with joy at his success" (John 3:29 LB).

Now he could have said to his disciples, "Why not get this Nazarene and bring him to me. We'll team up and join forces. Just think how many we can baptize. We'll form a corporation."

Not so with John. With unfeigned humility he answered, "He must become greater and greater, and I must become less and less" (John 3:30 LB).

If you don't think that's difficult to say and really mean, just try getting the words formed. It's terribly hard to utter, "I must become *less* and *less.*"

Man is just not geared to thinking in these terms. Instead we churn out the philosophy, "Do unto others *before* they do unto you." And above all, don't keep up with the Joneses—get ahead of them!

"I must become less and less." What humility! He said it, he meant it. John the Baptist—the man of the wilderness, the man of the dust, the man with the strange menu of milk, locusts, and honey has come down to us today as a great man who introduced Jesus Christ to the world. But here's the dilemma: How do you get humility and keep from taking great pride that you've become so humble?

Paul supplies our answer: "Don't be selfish; don't live to make a good impression on others. Be humble, thinking of others as better than yourself" (Philippians 2:3 LB). What a tendency we have to slip over those last seven words!

We're not born humble, that's for sure! From the time we're old enough to form sentences we're getting Mother's attention with, "Watch me," or, "See what I colored." And then there are those things we made and placed in a highly noticeable spot so that when someone did notice, we could nonchalantly say, "Oh, I made it," and hope they would shower praise on us.

In later years, our demand for attention demonstrates itself in our quest for the prestigious jobs, or through our unwillingness to serve in "lesser" places of honor.

Because of this innate pride, we have to work at humility, and it's hard work for most. Too many of us appear to enjoy singing (all too loudly), "Anything You Can Do I Can Do Better."

But God didn't say, *"Try* to be humble," or "Think of others the *same* as you would think of yourselves." He is specific and very definite. *Be humble. Think of others as better than yourself.*

No, achieving humility isn't easy, but it *is* possible. Sometimes I think Christians are secretly afraid to pray for genuine humility because we fear the experiences which God may use to make us humble. The temptation is to pray, "Lord, now I want you to give me humility. I really desire this. But, listen, don't make me look too bad, okay?"

We need not fear: God deals with us in love, and in His own time and in His own way, God can and does humble the willing Christian. The concept is emphasized by J. F. Strombeck, *(Disciplined by Grace): "Humility then is fostered by a deep sense of complete dependence upon God; by a realization of the infinitely glorious position in Christ. . . ."* It is our responsibility to ask for humility, and it is God's good pleasure to impart it. Coming from some of us, asking, in itself, must be a major accomplishment.

4

Listening—Watt's That You Said?

Athletic competition has always attracted me and I enjoy a keen desire to win. Therefore, it was a very strange experience to be playing table tennis with Barbara Spruill, a new friend, and realize that I had *no* desire to win! In analyzing the situation, I realized Barbara was responsible for my new attitude. As our friendship grew, I saw that I did not have to prove myself to her, nor did I have to be right. She would accept me regardless. In that I had known her only a short time, I wondered how she could have made me feel secure in our relationship so quickly.

Then, I noticed something else. When we disagreed, Barbara usually would say, "I could be wrong."

After hearing this several times, I asked, "Do you really think you might be wrong?"

She answered, "No, I really believe I'm right and you're wrong. However, there *is* a *possibility* I am wrong."

Always having the right answer doesn't make one stand taller. That's why Proverbs says: "Pride leads to arguments; be humble, take advice and become wise" (13:10 LB).

Many times I saw Barbara in a situation where she got no credit for the things she did. That bothered me—yet it *never* bothered her. She was not hung up with taking pride in her own accomplishments, and because she didn't attempt to feed her own ego, she spent her energy trying to build up someone else.

Along with her other good traits, Barbara has one quality so finely tuned I believe it may be her greatest attribute. She is a listener.

Most people feel what *they* have to say is the most important in a conversation, so they just tolerate the talk until they can interject their own words of wisdom again. But Barbara *talks* through listening. She communicates care in her eyes and expresses concern in her countenance. Apparently she knows very well the meaning of "A fool thinks he needs no advice, but a wise man listens to others" (Proverbs 12:15 LB). The longer I was around Barbara, the more I realized how much *I* needed to learn about listening—*really* listening.

One day while driving me to a singing engagement, Barbara was telling me a story. At intervals I would give a little grunt of acknowledgment. But one time after my *uh huh*, she suddenly stopped talking. When I looked up at her it was clear that she knew I hadn't been listening. I had uttered an approving *uh huh* when it should have been a sympathetic, "Oh, no!" I immediately asked her to forgive me for not giving her my full attention. I was not only inconsiderate, but my inattentiveness also implied that her conversation was not so important as my thoughts.

All along I had assumed I was a listening person, but then I began to remember other experiences which exposed my failure as a listener. Years ago Mother used to say, "If you're going to do something you know you shouldn't, don't hide it." I recall one afternoon when I was nine, I took her at her word. I found some cigarettes someone had left at the house. Since no one in our family smoked, I decided they mustn't go to waste. (I applied the principle: "Think about all the millions of starving children in India.") Unfortunately this particular day we had guests in the living room. My youngest sister, Swanee, and I proceeded to waltz into the room puffing away on our cigarettes. I could see the look of total disbelief on my mother's face, her eyes as big as saucers.

I'm afraid we had heard the implication of Mother's words, but not of her heart. We weren't listening to her basic *intention*. However, we did understand her intention when she got out the "board of education." We didn't need more schooling on *that* subject for some time, and I learned two important lessons: First, listen to the intention of a person's words, and second, smoking *can* be hazardous to your health—in more ways than one!

While words are used to transmit ideas and thoughts, they are not always adequate by themselves, because people don't always say what they mean—nor do they always mean what they say. For instance, many people take literally these words of a child, "I hate you," when the child is really saying, "Love me." Too often we hear the words but miss the meaning—sometimes intentionally.

It doesn't matter how many times a child is told, "Don't slam that door," or "Turn out that light," for he seems to become deaf at the most convenient times. Kids have an innocent habit of turning on lights and *leaving* them on, and we four were no exception.

I recall one talk my father had with us about electricity and its use (or overuse). He called us together and passed a piece of paper to each of us. On each paper were long lists of numbers and words which he commenced to read aloud. Dad had made a list showing what it cost to use each size light bulb, so we could see how much it cost per hour to have a light burning. For example:

> 1—100-watt bulb cost 4¢ to burn for 1 hour
> 1—150-watt bulb cost 6¢ to burn for 1 hour
> 1—200-watt bulb cost 8¢ to burn for 1 hour

I can still see us sitting there holding our papers while Dad very seriously went over the entire electrical system with us! I assure you, none of us laughed, yet we didn't take this wattage seminar too seriously either. Today, however, I find myself going around my own apartment turning off unnecessary lights; for now I get these friendly little bills each month addressed to me, not to Dad. To date, I have not worked out a deal with the Dallas Power and Light Company to furnish me with free sunshine. I also learned it was profitable to listen to Dad—in more ways than one!

I've just begun to discover some of the many dimensions of listening. How rare today to find a person with a listening ear! How easy to find someone with a motor mouth! God addresses both kinds: "A wise man holds his tongue. Only a fool blurts out everything he knows" (Proverbs 10:14 LB).

Proverbs is a most poignant book on wisdom, and I especially appreciate what it says about listening:

> The wise man learns by listening; the simpleton can learn only by seeing scorners punished.
>
> Proverbs 21:11 LB

> When there are many words, transgression is unavoidable, But he who restrains his lips is wise.
>
> Proverbs 10:19 NAS

> Don't talk so much. You keep putting your foot in your mouth. Be sensible and turn off the flow!
>
> Proverbs 10:19 LB

Please understand. God is not speaking just to incessant talkers: He is addressing *all of us* who talk when we should be listening. Sometimes we have to *look and listen* for an opportunity to minister to another through listening.

For example, a reporter for one of America's largest newspapers recently shared with me the fact that as a child she stuttered terribly. She was treated more like an ornament than a person, and her parents' attitude was, "Be quiet, a grown-up is speaking."

However, a sensitive neighbor next door welcomed her for afternoon visits. In the reporter's words, "With Mrs. Gibbons I not only sat and listened to her talk about the good old days, but I was aware that she actually listened to *me* as I'd talk on about school and dreams I had for my future. I noticed during the time

I spent with her I didn't stutter. I believe it was simply because I knew she was honestly listening to me. She showed me she cared by listening to what I had to say."

I seriously doubt that Mrs. Gibbons realized at the time the full and lasting impact she was to have on this child. Would this woman have predetermined that, by focusing her attention on this little girl, she, herself, would become part of a healing process in Jane's life? Probably not.

Many lonely people are near us wanting and needing someone to talk with—not to talk *to,* but to talk *with!* Just a couple of months ago I became aware of this fact after a man asked if he could talk with me about a problem. (In a counseling situation I believe you should never *tell* a person what you can *lead* him to discover for himself.)

He started with no hesitancy telling me about his problem. I just sat and listened and made no attempt to interrupt. After he'd talked about fifteen minutes he got up and said, "Thank you so much. You'll never know how much this has helped me."

When he had gone, I thought to myself, "Helped him! I didn't say a word." But then I realized that just by allowing him to express himself, I had made it possible for him to solve his own problem—or at least to be better prepared to solve it. Some people merely need sounding boards to test their ideas without fear or rejection or interruption. This experience validated my new awareness that listening to others is more than a ministry— *it is a necessity.*

When I was talking with a very successful businessman in Dallas not long ago, he shared that, outside of his wife, I was his only true friend. The reason he gave was, "You are the only other person who really listens to me." What a sad commentary on the human race. It is evident we spend more time tuned into television than we do to people.

Perhaps that partially explains the tremendous boom today in one particular field of science—psychiatry. Its growth is unparalleled; yet, are our basic needs today any different from those of people hundreds of years ago? No. Are we really ministering to each other by listening? No. As Gini Andrews points out in *Your Half of the Apple,* "Half the psychiatrists' couches in the world would be empty if there were more loving ears available."

Communication has been silenced in many families, and statistics are staggering, particularly concerning the percentage of American marriages today which are destined to fail. This was unheard of in times past. Communication is an essential ingredient in achieving a meaningful relationship.

If someone said to you, "I want you to communicate with Bob," what picture do you get in your mind? Pause just a moment. Who would do most of the talking? You? When the average person thinks of communicating with another person, he thinks of himself as doing the talking. However, communication is a *shared* experience. Listening is a language without words, a potent language all its own.

Dr. John W. Drakeford in his book *The Awesome Power of the Listening Ear* reveals the potency of listening. He says, "Listening is an art. Have this in mind if you aspire to be a competent listener. However, while artists are undoubtedly born, not made, they are certainly not born made. Laborious hours have polished the rough-hewn crystalline carbon of capacity until it shines in all its multifaceted diamond brilliance."

Even in our physical makeup we ought to get some clues as to the importance of listening. God gave us two ears and as Zeno, the Greek philosopher, put it, "We have two ears and one mouth that we may listen the more and talk the less."

If you would, picture Jesus in your mind with another person. Do you imagine Him doing all the talking? Personally, I see Jesus listening not only to the words of others, but also to their hearts.

The disciples on the road to Emmaus experienced this willingness of Jesus to listen. They were totally distraught over the events of the past week and were discussing their disappointments when a sensitive stranger joined the group.

Now Jesus knew that His disciples were all wrong in their

evaluation of the events concerning His death and Resurrection, but he encouraged them to pour out their doubt-filled disputations by asking: "What is this discussion that you are exchanging . . . as you walk along?" (Luke 24:17 AMPLIFIED).

And without interrupting one time, Jesus listened. Then, when they had finished their account, He patiently explained to them the dispensational dealings of God from Moses to Calvary, and they understood.

Sometimes people can't receive our tidbits of wisdom because their minds are too full; and if we will prayerfully minister to that person through listening, we can often be the instrument God can use to rid his heart of deep-seated bitterness and hurt, thus opening his mind to the dynamic, life-changing concepts of God's Word.

Jesus tells us in Matthew, "He that hath ears to hear, let him hear" (11:15), and Solomon states in Proverbs, "The wise man learns by listening . . ." (see 1:5). This brings to mind what I consider to be the loveliest, simplest prayer in the Bible. It's found in 1 Samuel: "Speak, Lord; for thy servant heareth" (see 3:9).

I pray I shall never forget this and that I'll never neglect saying this prayer before starting the day's activities. The impact of that Scripture and the potential it carries reach me. If we could all be as oriented to God's leadership as was Samuel, we would not only *hear* when He speaks, but would *act* on what He says.

Then James's words would have much more meaning and joy for us: "But be ye doers of the word, and not hearers only . . ." (1:22).

I confess: It has taken me years to learn a few basic lessons from God and I'm only beginning. The heart has ears and I am sure God has thought many times that June Hunt was hard of hearing.

God is not vague. His voice is clear and He is articulate. He tells us, "Be still, and know . . ." (Psalms 46:10). Oh, the things He wants to teach us—the things He wants us to know!

For example, if you were to fall overboard from a boat in the midst of a great lake, the wisest thing for you to do (if the boat is unreachable) is to be still. Relaxing, you would float and conserve energy. Desperately flailing and fighting the water would result in wasted energy which could cost you your life, but being still would allow you the opportunity to take stock of your situation and to make a decision as to the wisest course of action to follow. Listening to God is the key to inner peace.

Christ promised peace to His disciples, yet each one died a martyr's death except John. What happened to that promised peace? Had Jesus lied? No. We must understand *external peace* is totally different from *internal peace.* Jesus did not stand on some street corner passing out rose-colored glasses and promises of life without trials. His gift of peace was the ability to *be still,* to be at rest in a turning, churning world—peace in the midst of turmoil—peace that indeed surpasses all understanding. We have access to this peace when we begin listening to the voice of God.

God prefers to speak quietly to those who wait quietly to hear, and to those who wait to listen for the voice of God. Isaiah contains this powerful promise, "But they that wait upon the Lord shall renew their strength; they shall mount up with wings as eagles; they shall run, and not be weary; and they shall walk, and not faint" (40:31).

Yes, I'm just beginning to listen, but I can identify with the experience of a friend upon discovering Christ: "I heard, and I heard, and I heard, and I heard, then one day—I HEARD!"

5

Sensitivity—Jogging, Jingles, and Jesus

While visiting Huntsville, Alabama, I had the privilege of meeting the young woman who was to become Miss Alabama that year. She was director of a summer program for her church and asked if I would sing for the young people. I accepted the invitation happily.

Arrangements were made for me to borrow a guitar (which is like trying to cook in someone else's kitchen) as I did not have mine with me. I asked if the guitar were in tune and was assured that it was. As I began to play, I realized too late that "in tune" doesn't have the same meaning for everyone. I glanced at the two guitarists who had played before me; they gave me that "we've-been-there-too" look.

After the program was over, while in conversation with a group of people, I mentioned that I had not meant to start with the guitar out of tune. They looked puzzled—not one of them had noticed! Apparently, since they had not conditioned themselves to listen for fine tuning, they were not sensitive to the fact that the instrument was, indeed, out of tune.

Sensitivity is a quality which is *developed*. We are not born with it. Only after many years of experience in handling money can a teller identify a bill as counterfeit merely by touching it. Only after years of listening to music was I able to learn to tune a guitar to perfect pitch. And my speed and accuracy increased as the *intensity* of my attention was placed on the intervals between strings. I *developed* a sensitivity to pitch.

But what is "sensitivity" in relation to tuning a person's life? Sensitivity requires full concentration on another person's needs, wants, and desires. It means being in tune with his spirit and listening not only to the melody, but also to all the other notes making up his harmonic structure.

For example, how many times have we watched a person take a fall? Sometimes the fall looks funny and so we laugh. But the guy who fell isn't laughing. He's crying on the inside. He's crying for someone to stand by him. As we walk off we wonder, "Why doesn't someone offer to help?"

We've all done it. We've all been insensitive. Yet, we can explain!

"I don't have time to help."

"You never know what you're letting yourself in for when you get involved."

"It won't hurt to tell just a few people. After all, it's the *truth.*"

"He probably did something to deserve it, anyway."

Do any of these sound familiar? Oh, yes. Our rationalizing minds come quickly to our defense. Whatever happened to empathy—that participation in another person's feelings? What about getting into the other guy's shoes and traveling down *his* road?

It's interesting to consider that as Jesus Christ walked down a road, people would flock around Him. They came from all over just to be near Him. But why? Certainly not because of His looks, or clothes, or the clever things He said. According to Isaiah, "He has no stately form or majesty that we should look upon Him; nor appearance that we should be attracted to Him" (*see* 53:2 NAS). The people were drawn to Jesus because of His penetrating sensitivity which drew their hearts to Him. Jesus, as a mortal man, let the love of God flow through Him into the lives of those people. Even as He was betrayed, misunderstood, denounced, and crucified, He still continued to let God love *through* Him. He remained sensitive to the needs of people, and because they believed His *heart,* in turn, they believed His *words.* Few men today can comprehend such sensitivity.

One of the classic examples of sensitivity in the Bible is the account of the delicate way Jesus handled the situation with the woman at the well. This woman and everyone around her knew she had sinned.

However, after Jesus asked her about her husband, the woman (hedging around) tried to rationalize her answer. But she didn't have to answer, because by the look in His eyes and the few words He spoke, she knew she had been found out. If you have ever been "found out," you are aware it is one of the most sickening experiences we can know, and immediately we start building defenses in order to protect ourselves.

Now this woman at the well had been found out, but strangely enough she did not defend herself. Why? Not because of *her*, but because of *Him*—Jesus Christ. She was face-to-face with Jesus, and His tremendous sensitivity toward her broke down the potential barriers between them. Rather than judging, He loved; rather than seeing fault, He saw need. She had no cause for defensiveness because He allowed her nothing against which to defend.

We defend when there is an attack. In our judicial court system, before there is a need for a defense, there has to be an *accusation*, a *charge*, a *prosecution*. Defensiveness is a reaction word and because of Jesus' sensitivity to this woman, He gave her nothing to react against. The questionable action of another person should only serve as an incentive to ask, "*Why?* What need is crying out?" If we seek to find out the *why* of people's actions, we'll get answers. And it is on the *why* level that we can deal most effectively.

This woman's promiscuity was merely a *symptom* of a great need. Jesus overlooked her previous actions and went to where these actions originated—her heart. Jesus knew well that *when hearts change, actions change.*

Service to God through sensitivity may take many forms—one being unselfish service to others. A very personal example of this occurred on one special gift-buying day at the time my sister

Helen was planning to be married. I wanted my wedding gift to her to be something practical—but fun, too. While walking through a department store one day, I spotted the most unusual luggage I had ever seen. This attractive set almost said, "Buy me!" The luggage was a striking black and white pattern of abstract flowers with a dazzling orange interior. The total effect was very chic.

Well, I bought it and did I ever make a real production of Helen's gift! I stacked the luggage, one piece on top of the other, and then covered it all with a sheet. When I gave it to Helen, I unveiled my gift with three times the flourish of a Michelangelo revealing his magnificent David!

I knew Helen really liked the gift and I guess she realized I liked it, too, because several months later, I borrowed a piece of her luggage for a short trip. Upon reaching my destination I found that grains of rice had snuggled between my clothing—leftovers of her August honeymoon. I knew how much sentimental attachment she must have placed on the luggage, and I was thrilled that my gift could have been a part of the honeymoon.

When Christmas came that year we were all excited because a special spirit is always present at our family gatherings. Among the presents for me was a jingle from Helen which read:

> A gift for you, my sister, June
> For you I'd buy the sun and moon,
> I know some luggage to you is a hit
> And so I'd like to let you have it.
> Use it well and you'll look hip,
> And think of me on every trip.

And there it was—the *very* set I had given her! That, undoubtedly, was one of the most meaningful gifts I could have received, and even *more*—a real lesson in giving. Of course, Helen could have called the store and told them to send out an identical set; but instead, she gave me the very pieces I had given her. I asked her later why she did it that way and she answered, "June, it wouldn't have been enough to give you a gift *like* mine. I wanted to give you *the* gift you gave me." In doing so, she gave me a part of herself. Helen demonstrated real sensitivity by thinking more about my desires than her own, and I'll never forget the motive and love behind her action.

Now at airports everywhere, my luggage is easily recognizable. My suitcases are the ones with the big flowers on them, but more than that, they are the ones with the love and heart of my sister stamped invisibly on them. Because of her sensitive, unselfish gift, Helen goes with me everywhere. I know her prayers do, too, and that luggage is a constant reminder of true giving and love.

When I am not giving that luggage a good workout (which is seldom), I occasionally work out myself. I often jog for a mile to tone up my body. Usually I jog without stopping (my friends say I expend more energy going up and down than forward), but one morning after the initial ten yards my muscles seemed to lose their strength. I spotted a curb ahead so I thought I'd start walking at that point and pick up the jogging later.

I noticed a woman walking her dog and when I got closer, she turned toward me and called, "I want you to know how much I admire you because I know how hard that must be." (I don't exactly make jogging look easy.)

I was almost to that curb, when suddenly I became aware that I was actually picking up my speed as well as my feet. As I turned the next corner I was amazed. Somehow this woman had exhorted me to keep going without even realizing it.

The ministry we can have in the lives of other people through exhortation is tremendous, but what does *exhort* mean? Bragging on someone for the sake of making him feel better? Or feeding someone's ego?

Webster states: *exhort*—to advise earnestly; *exhortation*—language intended to encourage.

That word *encourage* is the key word. We are told by Jesus to

"Love one another" and pure love by its own nature is encouraging. If one grows in sensitivity and love toward God, he cannot help but love and encourage others. I'm always amazed how God handles things. In the common happenstance of a woman walking her dog, God helped me understand another facet of sensitivity.

The Mooneys, in turn, taught me that realizing a person's intent is also a form of sensitivity. These friends lived in our neighborhood and one of my favorite activities as a child was to climb upon Dr. Mooney's knee and have him read out of my giant green storybook. By democratic process, we voted on our choice of stories. (The doctor read *Little Black Sambo* most of the time, since mine was the only vote that counted.)

One day I learned Dr. Mooney had broken his leg. Well, I just had to do something, so my little, chubby fingers picked a small cluster of flowers. I was so proud I thought my heart would burst with excitement as I ran to his door. When his wife came I exclaimed, "These are for Dr. Mooney." I noticed a surprised look on her face. I figured Dr. Mooney would be surprised, too —and was he ever! They made me feel like I had just given them the crown jewels of England.

However, many years later I found out I had plucked the Mooney's *prizewinning* flowers! They never let me know. They were so sensitive to my child's heart, they never thought of squelching the enthusiastic giving of a little girl whose *intentions* were good. I thank God for their sensitivity, for they could have shattered my childish joy of giving and replaced it with fear.

Many people react before considering the basic intent. From a tenderhearted doctor I have come to realize that all the libraries in the world could not contain those words—words that never would have been spoken if the basic intent had first been considered.

6

Methods—Right or Wrong

How many times have we seriously set out to accomplish something—but in a wrong way? We realize too late that if we had handled a certain situation differently, in the *right* way, we would have saved much time, emotion, and energy. But how can we know which way is right?

The only sure way I know is to let God *tell* us what is the right way. As Proverbs 3:5,6 states, "Trust in the Lord with all your heart, And do not lean on your own understanding. In all your ways acknowledge Him, And He will make your paths straight" (NAS).

It is so important that we listen to the Lord rather than to logic alone, because He is not limited to just one *logical* way of doing things. As Paul says to the Corinthians, "God has deliberately chosen to use ideas the world considers foolish and of little worth . . ." (1 Corinthians 1:27 LB), the ultimate purpose being that our lives should have an impact on people—not necessarily the whole world—but certainly upon those with whom we come in contact daily. And since God *alone* understands the totality of the situation and the variables of human behavior, He must choose the method through which to work. For while our *first* reaction is to face life with our tool of logic, we must use God's Word as the basis of our action.

We are often led *astray* when we react in what seems to be the *logical* way, as in the case of Simon Peter. In the Garden of

Gethsemane, Judas (the betrayer) entered, bringing with him soldiers, police, and Pharisees to arrest Jesus. Alarmed that the Lord's life was threatened, Peter, not particularly noted for patience, grabbed his sword and slashed off the right ear of Malchus, one of the mob. This bold, brawny fisherman was ready to fight off every man in the garden in order to protect his Master!

Peter's actions, from one point of view, have to be admired. His intentions were *good;* but his rash actions were against everything Jesus had taught. It was really hard for him to understand the rebuke Jesus gave, and it was with great reluctance that Peter put away his sword, still *believing* that his act was justified—was logical!

Again, we must realize that *right* things can be done *wrong.* The fact that Peter wanted to save the Lord was not *wrong,* but the way he chose to do so was not *right.*

In contrast, every Christian knows the joy of an experience where the Lord has taken some act of obedience which seemed illogical at the time and blessed it to a surprising degree.

I doubt that the boy with the loaves and fishes could have ever predicted the far-reaching results of his obedience. You will remember that the people had come from miles around to hear Jesus speak. The hillside was a collage of color and faces of the people who sat waiting. Surprisingly, most had not brought any food with them that day.

Jesus, knowing their humanness, asked Philip what should be done about feeding the large crowd. After pointing out to Jesus that there was not enough money to take care of food, Philip couldn't come up with any solution.

Now Jesus had a number of alternatives available to Him. He could have:

—sent everyone home to eat, or
—taken up a collection to buy food, or
—asked several rich men to underwrite the cost of the meal, or
—multiplied the money and sent Philip to bring back the food, or
—made the money or the food itself appear out of nothing.

Yet Jesus did none of these, for a small boy offered to give up his loaves and two fishes.

Can you imagine the people's initial response when they saw the lad offer his lunch to feed the thousands? How funny . . . how ridiculous . . . how stupid! Oh, Jesus must have smiled at the little boy—not because the offer was absurd, but because of the pleasure He must have felt at seeing a child give *all he had.*

The story of the multiplying of the bread and fish is well known. The quantity was so great that they had twelve baskets of food left over. Yes, this was one of Jesus' most graphic miracles, and it is the one most people remember best, but perhaps the real miracle lies within the heart of the boy who gave everything he had to Jesus. That really amazes me because it seems little boys are always hungry. Therefore, the natural thing for him would have been to keep at least one roll and a few bites of fish for himself.

Through some divine insight withheld even from the disciples, this child moved from a realm of logic to a realm of obedience.

There's also another lesson to learn from this episode. Jesus *involved* people and made them a *part* of His miracle. He could have snapped His fingers and food would have fallen from heaven. Instead, Christ chose to take a small boy and a small amount of food and go from there—because through this method everyone there was a part of Jesus' miracle. *Every single person* who ate a morsel of food was *involved* as a vital member of the multiplying story.

The Christian life is one of addition, not subtraction. God can take the most minute thing and make it a useful instrument for His work. It doesn't make sense to rule out as unworkable something that God says, just because it doesn't seem logical in *our* minds.

In my experience as youth director, I saw continuous results through group projects, and I worked hard to be aware of opportunities to share seemingly "illogical" projects on the one-to-one level.

One of these opportunities occurred through a fifteen-year-old boy who tried very hard to be tough. I had heard about some illegal transactions he had made with fellow students at his school. Although I didn't know if the report was true, I did know he was having problems getting along with his family. When I spotted him one day, I said, "I've got a project I want you to help me with."

"What is it?" he asked, proud he'd been singled out. I asked him to meet me in my office at 3 P.M. when I would explain.

Deliberately, I made him wait until then so he would arrive with some degree of anticipation. True to my expectation, he arrived fifteen minutes early. To start our conversation, I told him about a course I had taken called the Institute in Basic Youth Conflicts, where the instructor told a true story about a girl he had worked with who was faced with a dilemma: if she told her parents about her decision to become a Christian she wouldn't be permitted to go to church, however, if she *lied* about where she was going, then she could sneak off to church.

The instructor referred us to 1 Thessalonians 5:18 which says, "In every thing give thanks: for this is the will of God in Christ Jesus concerning you" (which in the natural sense is *totally* illogical!). Not "in every *good* thing" nor "in every *Christian* thing" but "in *every* thing give thanks." The *in* does not mean everything that happens to you is *caused* by God; rather, through all things give thanks because God is going to teach you things through those experiences which may not have been learned otherwise.

The girl went home, told her mother she had become a Christian, and asked if she could go to church that night. The enraged mother said no, so the girl silently thanked God for the response and then asked her mother if there was anything she could do around the house to help. Although shocked by her daughter's response, she said the dishes needed to be done. After the kitchen was cleaned up, the daughter returned to ask if there was anything else she could do. Her mother, stunned by the changed spirit, told her she could go to church but that she would have to be back by nine. God changed her mother's mind because the daughter had let God be God in her life—she had given the problem to Him.

After relating the story, I confided to the boy, "I was thinking about teaching this principle of thanking God through everything to our group, but I want to know first if you think it works."

He said, "Yeah, I guess so."

"Great!" I exclaimed. "Well, this is where you come in. I want you to try it and let me know how you come out."

"Oh, no!" he objected, "not me." But after several minutes of discussion, he promised at least to think about it.

When he left, I thought that was probably the end of that. Yet, two nights later I saw my "project" heading my way in true Batman form. Leaping (unsuccessfully) over the hundreds of chairs between us, he breathlessly exclaimed, "It works. It works!" In almost inaudible gulps he continued, "After talking with you, I went home and told Mom I got a morning job at the skating rink, but she said I couldn't take it. So I just said, 'Thank You, Lord.' Then I cleaned up my room and when I came downstairs, Mom said I could go!"

That was great. Firsthand, he had learned what could happen if his response was right. But I did want to make sure about this story, so I phoned his mother. After exchanging a few pleasantries I said, as nonchalantly as I could, "Tell me, how is the family?"

In a half whisper she said, "Well, to tell you the truth, my husband and I can't figure out what's happened to our son. Normally, if we say we won't let him do something, he goes on a silence strike. Yet the other night he accepted it beautifully. And you won't believe this—he asked if I wanted him to vacuum his room! He cleaned the entire upstairs for an hour and a half!

"Actually, the only reason I didn't want him at the skating rink was because our out-of-town relatives were coming for a week and I was going to need him to help out. But that night he did so much I didn't need him the next morning. And I figured if he took the other children skating each morning, it would help immensely."

Three years later I saw this boy again and instantly remembered our experiment. I asked him if he still used the project of thanking God when irritated.

"Well," he answered rather sheepishly, "not as often as I should." But then he looked me squarely in the eyes and said, "But, when I do, it works!"

He said it *all* in those last two words. If we let God use *His power* in our lives, continually thanking Him through *everything*, it really works.

It's so foolish to expect God to confine Himself to logical ways of doing things; and He refuses to be hemmed in by the realm of our understanding. When Moses was sandwiched between the Red Sea and a pursuing Egyptian army, the logical thing to have done would have been to raise the white flag; in fact, a caucus was held in support of this move. Or, he could have called out the engineers to draw some quick sketches for some sort of bridge.

But Moses realized that there was time to do only one thing. Pray! Can you imagine the people's disgust when Moses, after praying, explained that he was going to get them out of the situation by stretching out a rod over the Red Sea? This was *totally* illogical and the situation was far too grave for fun and games. But to their utter amazement, the waters rolled back, and across they ran.

And today, through obedience (drab word that it is) even to those commandments which "seem" illogical, we are given the exciting opportunity to see the Lord God Himself at work. What a sight! *When God takes over the end justifies the means.* How illogically logical!

7

God's Timing—Watch Out!

Everybody has had the experience of planting something and waiting impatiently for it to grow—such was my third-grade experience with carrots. I planted some in our backyard, and I thought my hair would turn gray before I finally saw the green tops breaking through the soil. Then Mother explained, "Just as *you* need time to grow, so do they. Be patient and don't bother them. I'll tell you when they're ready."

I thought I'd pull up just *one* carrot; however, that one was so small, I pulled up two more to see how *they* were doing. They weren't. So, I replanted my baby carrots and decided to take my mother's advice. Weeks later, when we dug up all the carrots, my heart sank into my shoes. My recycled trio hadn't just failed to grow, they were shriveled up and deformed!

As a third grader, the only lesson I learned was, "It's not nice to fool Mother Nature," and you certainly can't rush her. Her timing on all living things is perfect and we are not to tamper with, or hinder, that timing. As an adult I see the lesson from another perspective. I had destroyed those carrots because I had interfered with God's timing. My impatience (as most times it is) was a *destroyer*.

Before this realization, I used to wear myself out trying to change His timing. For instance, while still in high school, I prayed for a year and a half that God would make a way for me to go to Baylor University. There seemed to be something special about the lives of some of the kids I knew who were going there. However, I knew my father wanted me near home, attending Dallas's Southern Methodist University—which is about as close as you can get. So I prayed, "God, I know You can do it. Make Dad say yes." Dad said *no*. Now, that was only strike one against me and I wasn't about to give up that easily.

For entrance requirements, SMU demanded the Standard Achievement Tests while Baylor utilized the American College Testing Scores. My plot was simple: I would go at a snail's pace during the SAT, and then SMU would not accept me. Then all that would remain would be the ACT and I would be batting a thousand.

However, the night before I took the ACT, our school's annual musical was premiering and, because I was president of the choir, I had been up until 3:00 A.M. finishing all the last-minute details for the show. That morning I did something I had never done. I fell asleep through part of the test.

My Rip van Winkle stunt didn't bother me, though, because in my junior year I had taken the tests and apparently had done well enough to warrant a letter from Baylor. I was offered honors classes in two out of four categories. They mistakenly thought I was a senior.

So, true to my game plan, I bombed the SAT. My final effort was to write four sentences on the SMU application in answer to "Why do you wish to attend SMU?"

1. I do not wish to attend SMU.
2. My college preference is elsewhere.
3. My father merely wishes me to apply.
4. I prefer to be rejected.

I felt so smug with my four-point system and my sophisticated phraseology that I was not ready for the fast ball thrown to me just a few days later—a letter of acceptance to good old SMU! Strike two! However, I still wasn't out, but I never expected the curve I was to receive a week following the SMU letter—a letter of rejection from good old Baylor. My ACT score had not been adequate for acceptance. It seems I was so busy making z-z-z's I failed to make an *A*. I struck out! I couldn't understand it. I just *knew* Baylor was where God wanted me to go. After all, it is, *"My will be done,"* isn't it?

I entered SMU with my personal philosophy, "Make the best of all situations or they'll get the best of you" (1 June 3:16). Surprisingly enough, honors began coming to me early in my freshman year and continued until I graduated. The entry of my name in *Who's Who in American Colleges and Universities*, and receiving the most coveted award for outstanding contribution, and other honors, along with my happiness at SMU, served as a verification that God had spoken to me through my father.

I really majored in extracurricular activities, but they didn't have a tassel that color for graduation, so I walked in line with all the music majors. The experience I gained working in varied organizations with people of different backgrounds laid the foundation for me in my future work. But I didn't know it at the time. God knew what He was doing all along. Even though I didn't receive an M.R.S. degree (as I assumed I would), I did walk away with a Bachelor of Music. (Yes, I was still a bachelor but I prefer to call myself an unclaimed blessing!)

After completing a year of postgraduate courses, the pastor of the First Baptist Church of Dallas, Dr. W. A. Criswell, called me to his study. He wanted me to join his staff as the junior-high director. Never having *considered* attending a seminary or being a youth director, I was astonished! After all, this wasn't like teaching a beginner Sunday-school class. He was asking me to head a division of six hundred fifty students in the world's largest southern Baptist church.

Immediately I knew God wanted me to accept the position, so I did; however, my heart didn't want it. The peculiar thing is that usually you know God wants you to do a certain thing because you feel joy about it, but to be perfectly honest, when I walked away I was really down.

I remembered being puzzled over this Scripture: "Delight thyself also in the Lord; and he shall give thee the desires of thine heart" (Psalms 37:4). I wondered about this statement because I knew that the desires of our hearts aren't always right. After thinking about it awhile it dawned on me that God *changes* those desires of ours which are not good for us—*if* we let Him. As we delight ourselves in Him, He changes our desires to be what they *should* be.

But how do you delight yourself in the Lord, or, for that matter, in any person? You spend time talking with Him, listening to Him, putting His desires ahead of your own, doing things to please Him—even when you'd rather not. *You spend time.* And so I was learning and God was working. He did indeed change the desires of my heart. Ten weeks later I wouldn't have traded jobs with anyone. It was God's timing again.

As I assumed my responsibilities, I went into shock. Junior High Division! Nothing to it! All I had to do to be successful was be an *expert* in the fields of drama, journalism, counseling, multimedia, camping, advertising, and public relations. And, of course, there were those banquets, parties, fellowships, retreats, Bible studies, newspapers, annuals, and mission projects I would have to mastermind. Oh! And don't forget the guitar lessons and washtub band!

During the first year as youth director, I barely kept my head above water and I was continually exhausted. The second year I reasoned that I'd swum this course once—I could do it again. The third year I didn't even need to tread water once—I felt completely in control. The fourth year? Well, this one surprised me. Although I was swimming consistently and the work had never gone better, I felt a restlessness which I couldn't explain. After I had described this to Nadine Saucier, one of the most remarkable women I know, she said, "Restless? Oh, that's good. But you'd better get ready for a change."

"What do you mean?" I questioned.

She clarified that: "Two things will cause a restless spirit: one is unconfessed sin, but if you know it's not that, you can be *sure*

God is going to make a change in your life."

"But how do you figure that?" I persisted.

Then it became as clear as pure water when she elaborated: "God will not call you to move without preparing you. If God wanted you to move, yet everything was great and you did *not* feel restless, how would you know? This is only one of the ways He works to prepare us."

Sure enough, six weeks later I was made director of the church's six-hundred-member college and career division, and then I began to realize how God had prepared me *in His time, in His way* for *everything* I'd done. Those five years are invaluable ones to me and I treasure every memory I have of my work there. I learned to do things I never knew I could do, and whenever I said to myself, "Well, I don't know how to do that," I would remember my dad's words, *"so learn."*

He had spoken them the summer after my senior year in college. Dad decided I ought to go to Chicago to start a patriotic youth program and get adult sponsors. I said, "Well, Dad, I don't know anybody in Chicago."

He answered, "Well, find out who's there!"

"But I don't know how," I defended.

"So, go and learn," was his reply.

So I went and I learned. Somehow I arranged to be interviewed on television and radio to get the program publicized. I remember one day when I returned to my hotel a newspaper reporter asked, among other questions, "How much did you tip the cab driver?" I truthfully confided that by the time I had paid the fare, I had only seven cents left in my purse. The next morning the huge caps of the *Chicago Sun-Times* read, "Daughter of Millionaire Gives Cabbie Seven-Cent Tip."

This incident turned into a wire story and I got messages about it from all around the country. I also got one very pointed message from Dallas saying, "Come home." It's true, I had asked God to get me out of Chicago and (sooner than I had thought) I was heading back to Dallas. Ironically, Dad was providing the exit.

Obviously my dad was not the type to take *no* for an answer. When he told you to do something, you did it. This was really a blessing in disguise for I've learned many things from him because I *had* to. I had no choice. If you didn't know how to do some things, you found out.

Reflecting on my approach toward life, I believe I've learned more from my experiences with my father than anyone else. While my mother has had a tremendous impact on my life, Dad had forced me to be creative by always looking for new ways of doing things. He demanded more and he got more. Yet he challenged not only me, but the whole family.

Many factors have kept us from being an "average" family; however, there are many ways in which we are very average.

Two statements I've heard over and over during my lifetime are, one, "I'd give anything in the world to trade places with you"; and, two, "I wouldn't trade places with you for anything in the world."

It really doesn't make any difference what one would or would not trade: the fact remains we do not have the choice to do either. What makes the difference is how an individual *responds* to his own situation. *Either he responds to its positive influence or wallows in its negativism.*

Why shouldn't we let God be Creator *through* us as well as *of* us, by responding positively to irreversible situations and letting God teach us creativity within them? Again it's the battle of letting God *be* God in our lives.

8

Freedom—And the Lack of It

My father tried to instill in me the value of freedom, but he didn't stop with me, or my family.

On our sloped front lawn stands a forty-two-foot-high flagpole from which daily flies the American flag. At the base of the pole is a huge spotlight that illumines the stars and stripes at night. On the other side of our lawn is a large tree in which hundreds of white lights twinkle. Dad's explanation for the tree lights was always quick: "You see, someone passing by on the street might not see the flag at first, but they'll see the lighted tree and then their attention will be drawn to the flag. It's important they see the flag."

He was always concerned that there would be enough wind for it to unfurl and wave, and because of his loyalty taught me how to love that flag and what it represents!

I know my own sense of patriotism was greatly enhanced when Carolyn Gilbeaux (a college friend) and I went to Europe after my junior year. A student group of nineteen Americans made up our tour.

Carolyn and I were the adventurers. We believed that in order to get to know a country, we needed to know the people. We knew a smattering of languages, but together did well to get one sentence of a language correct between us.

Our trip took us into several Communist countries: East

Germany, Hungary, Czechoslovakia, and Yugoslavia. The scores of churches in West Berlin that still had bullet scars marring the exteriors made the war become more real to me than ever before. All the stories I had read about World War II and Germany came alive, and then I remembered hearing what a German had said, reflecting on his attitude during World War II.

> In Germany they came first for the Communists,
>   And I did not speak up because I was not a Communist.
> Then they came for the Jews,
>   And I did not speak up because I was not a Jew.
> Then they came for the Trade Unionists,
>   And I did not speak up because I was not a Trade Unionist.
> Then they came for the Catholics,
>   And I did not speak up because I was a Protestant.
> Then they came for me,
>   And by that time there was no one left to speak up.
>
>   MARTIN NIEMOELLER

Just before we were to leave West Berlin, we had an opportunity to climb a scaffold overlooking the Berlin Wall. I noticed a man on the platform frantically waving a white handkerchief. Looking past the rows of barbed wire and the steel barriers in the field, we saw a woman on the street about one hundred fifty yards away. From time to time she would hold up her baby for the man to see and then wave a handkerchief back at him. Our small group watched in hushed reverence.

Tears streamed from the man's eyes as he watched the woman and child reluctantly back away and slowly disappear out of sight. He had stood and watched the two of them until he was staring at an empty street. What total emptiness we all felt in that moment! What did *we personally* know about freedom—or the lack of it? Through the brief experience of a nameless man from another country, the value I placed on freedom multiplied before my eyes.

The incident was still fresh on our minds as our tour took us into other parts of East Germany. But as we approached the city of Pilsen, I suddenly felt very ill. So while the group got off the bus at the town square for refreshments, Carolyn and I stayed aboard. Shortly, Carolyn became aware of a man peering in the windows. She cautiously approached him and they began talking.

I could not hear what they were saying, so I got up and joined them. The man, speaking in broken English, said that before the Communist take-over he had been an engineer; but afterward he was forced to be a laborer in a coal mine. He had once owned his home; however, he now had to pay rent to live in the same house while sharing it with six other families. He had fought for freedom and he had lost it.

I will never forget his face. As we talked, he nervously continued to look behind as if afraid someone would catch him conversing with us. However, he explained his reason for taking the chance: he saw the English lettering on the bus, and wanted to talk with someone who could speak English.

Out of curiosity, I asked him if he had a Bible. With his head bowed he slowly related, "I write many letters to get Bible but no get. I write Canada—I know my letter get through. I not get. I try years to get one Bible."

At this point I left Carolyn talking to him and went to the back of the bus, and taking a New Testament bound in white from my purse I thought, "I can't give *this* one away. It was given to me by a special friend. It's too dear to me."

I looked around the bus to see if I could find an extra Bible somewhere. Then I thought, "June, what a giving spirit you have! Here this man has been trying to get a Bible for years and you hesitate!" I stood holding this Bible, still trying to convince myself it belonged to me; then finally I walked back to the man, held the Bible out to him through the window and said, "Here, I want you to have this."

He protested at first, saying, "No, I not take *your* Bible."

Before I knew it, I was saying, "Please take it. We can get all the Bibles we want in America."

Finally he carefully and tenderly took the Bible from me and just held it close. Then he opened the Bible at random and read with careful deliberation, "Blessed are they which are persecuted for righteousness' sake: for their's is the kingdom of heaven" (Matthew 5:10). The chill bumps came. Carolyn and I sat in total awe.

"Blessed are ye, when men shall revile you, and persecute you, and shall say all manner of evil against you falsely, for my sake (5:11).

"Rejoice, and be exceeding glad: for great is your reward in heaven: for so persecuted they the prophets which were before you" (5:12).

Tears welled up in his eyes, but he continued reading with his index finger underlining every word. When he finished, he took his billfold out of his pocket. "This is all I have," he whispered reverently. I tenderly unfolded the miniature parchment and read "Thy word is a lamp unto my feet, and a light unto my path" (Psalms 119:105). He would not keep my Bible until I would agree to keep his.

Here I had hesitated to give him just part of a Bible, one of many I owned. Yet he had given me *all* he had—one verse of one chapter of the one and only Bible he owned.

For the first time in my life I was able to understand with my *heart* what David meant in Psalms, "O how love I thy law!" (119:97) and, "The law of thy mouth is better unto me than thousands of gold and silver" (119:72). Even though this East German still had his same struggles to contend with, you'd have thought we'd given him the greatest of all treasures.

Accepting Christ into our lives doesn't take away our sorrows. Christ wants to reach deep within our souls to give us the calm assurance and ability to endure all things no matter how painful. I feel this hymn sums it up:

When peace, like a river, attendeth my way,
When sorrows like sea billows roll;
Whatever my lot, Thou has taught me to say,
It is well, it is well with my soul.

H.G. SPAFFORD

If anyone understood the heart of this message, that German Christian did.

God doesn't waste one single experience. The secret is the constant awareness of His desire to work *through* us, and work He can and will if our lives remain open to Him. The issue is not how *we feel* about our circumstances or other people, but a matter of looking at life from God's point of view. The entire perspective changes and *vision becomes much more than just sight.*

9

Adversity—Joy Is Not an Electric Blanket

Nighttime holds a strange fascination for me. While I used to assume one could see farther in daylight, I now believe *darkness is necessary* for seeing the longest distance. In fact, the darker the night the clearer God's universe appears: One can see planets and stars millions of miles *past* the sun.

I wonder, too, if I would fully appreciate the light of the day and the warmth of the sun if I had not known the dark coldness of the night. There are many things I would not value had I not been through periods of darkness. Truthfully, I value the hurts and difficulties in my own life much more than my successes. That's why it means so much to me when I sing the song, "Would You?" in which the words of Grace Hawthorne capture the light of darkness:

> Would you cherish loving arms if you'd never shed a tear?
> Would you welcome going home if you'd never been away?
> Would you treasure guiding hands if you'd never been alone?
> I don't think so,
> I really don't think so.
>
> Would you value having hope if you'd never known despair?
> Would you treasure being safe if you'd never lost your way?
> Would you cherish gentle words if you'd never been afraid?
> I don't think so,
> I really don't think so.

If we knew all the love that the Lord has shown to man,
If we really try to do what the Lord has planned for us,
Then we'd love each other more. We would find new happiness.
Yes, I think so,
I really do think so.

It takes tears, loneliness, desperation, and fear to realize the value of the *remedy* for all these—Jesus Christ.

A friend of mine who has experienced more than her share of adversity said this to me, "I sometimes think Christians are like teabags: you never know what kind you are until you get in hot water."

When you become a Christian, you give your whole life to Christ and an exchange occurs: You get *freedom* in life. Will difficulties still come your way? You can know they will! However, there is *freedom* from problems: a problem may still exist but you will not be *consumed* by it. Giving your *life* to Christ means your *problems, fears, loneliness, adversities*—*all* go to Him. They are not yours alone anymore.

It says in 1 Peter that followers of Christ shall be persecuted. For a man who is trying to attract followers, it seems strange that he would say, ". . . if you do right and suffer for it, and are patient beneath the blows, God is well pleased. This suffering is all part of the work God has given you" (2:20, 21 LB). Why would this be said even if it were true? Surely this wouldn't attract followers. After all, being a Christian in the first century wasn't exactly like going on an outing to the zoo. Membership in the Lions Club then didn't hold the distinction it does today.

God sees things from an overall perspective. He sees us in our rough, unpolished state, yet knows all the while what we could be *worth*. "Life is a grindstone; whether it grinds a man down or polishes him up depends on the kind of stuff he's made of."

Unpleasantries of any kind can be used by God as effective chisels to chip off and refine our rough spots. The man who is willing to let the Creator *finish* His work to perfection will see definite changes in his life.

Every person is very special to God, for regardless of the value you place on yourself, He places an even higher value on you. He knows the potential within you and how it can best be used.

God requires our "readiness" to suffer. I like to think of God's dealings with man as analogous to a surgeon. In the *natural* an operation is the most cruel, heartless thing a doctor could do to another human. However, the surgeon must inflict pain at times so that the diseased parts of the body can be removed and the healing processes can begin. We endure the *pain* because we trust the *over-all results.*

Carved into the famous Black Hills of South Dakota are the gigantic faces of four past United States presidents. When asked how he could have sculpted the figures on such a huge scale, the craftsman replied, "It was simple. I just chipped away the pieces I didn't need. The faces were there all the time."

The greatness is in *you* all the time. The potential is there, awaiting God's work in our lives—the work of chipping away the rough edges of our lives so we can accomplish the *purpose* for which we were created. *God never made a nobody.*

Through the book *The Cost of Discipleship,* Dietrich Bonhoeffer has done much to show me that there literally can be *joy in suffering.* I like the way The Living Bible paraphrases Matthew 5:11: "When you are reviled and persecuted and lied about because you are my followers—wonderful!"

This certainly was the way Bonhoeffer felt about serving Jesus Christ, for his life was a monumental example of overcoming the world. Bonhoeffer was a young German Christian very disturbed about the church during the Nazi regime in Germany. The church had been a laughing matter in the face of the rising Nazi power.

Bonhoeffer writes, "Cheap grace is the problem. Grace without discipleship is grace without the cross." Nobody listened to Bonhoeffer's cries to continue to follow Christ and many of his church friends went over to Hitler's side. Bonhoeffer openly denounced Hitler and, of course, was soon jailed as a conspirator, but even in prison he remained a joyous Christian and wrote to friends, "You must never doubt that I am thankful and glad to go the way in which I am being led."

In 1945, Bonhoeffer was executed, just a few days before the Allied Liberation. Through it all he left a legacy—by not bemoaning his situation or playing martyr. As he practiced, "In *everything* give thanks," Bonhoeffer inspired hundreds of thousands to consider living life to the fullest measure.

Probably no one has better summed up Bonhoeffer's commitment to Jesus Christ than Bonhoeffer himself when he wrote, "And if we answer the call to discipleship, where will it lead us? What decisions and partings will it demand? To answer these questions, we will have to go to Him for only He knows the answer. Only Jesus Christ, who bids us follow Him, knows the journey's end. But we do know that it will be a road of boundless mercy. Discipleship means *joy.*"

What a Christ we follow! To be able to give a man peace, excitement, and joy in the face of death.

Bonhoeffer's imprisonment and death was never Hitler's victory. Bonhoeffer was relentlessly the victor. And because of that triumphant life, untold numbers have come to a personal relationship with this man's Lord.

Remarks made by the many returned prisoners of the Viet Nam war are very impressive. One former POW spoke repeatedly of the power of prayer and the faith that was abundant in the prison camps.

Captain Alex B. Aronis, who was involved in a ministry to returning POWs at Subic Bay Naval Air Station in the Philippines, related, "The key to their survival and to their mental and emotional health was a deep, abiding relationship with God.

"The story of the religious experiences of these men is inspiring beyond words," he continued. "One man told me that without God he would not have been able to survive. I asked him if he meant that God really helped the POWs and he said, 'No, not merely helped. I meant it when I said I could not have made it without God pulling me through!' The religious experience was so significant and so beneficial for some," Aronis wrote, "that two that I know of said they were *glad* they had the prison experience because of *what they learned in terms of life, values, and priorities.*"

We don't have to spend time in prison to know enslavement. A disturbing number of people walking around today are less free than these POWs. "Iron bars do not a prison make," and too many individuals are living in solitary confinement, separated from the only One who can give real freedom.

Having freedom involves a search—an honest search for God. I must truthfully say that to me there is not a more meaningful verse in the Bible than, "If you seek me, you *will find me* when you *search* for me with *all your heart*" (*see* Jeremiah 29:13).

Those words "will find me" are a promise of God. Yes, a *promise!* The only condition is *search with an open heart.* It is *His* responsibility to reveal Himself to us.

Then, as we are free to know our Creator, we in turn are free to know His creation—to know ourselves. Thus, when the iron bars of man's limitations and expectations are removed from our souls, we can fly as far and as high as the heavens. And, at the same time, we are free to see ourselves as we really are . . . free to give our imperfect *real* selves to an imperfect world of real needs.

10

Message Music—Reach Out and Touch

How would you feel if you were driving a $100,000 racing car, you were only minutes away from winning one of the largest purses in auto racing, you were in the lead on the last lap, and you ran out of gas?

I watched this actually happen in the Pocono 500, one of the biggest races of the 1973 season, and I couldn't believe my eyes. The fault, of course, lay in the lack of proper planning.

Undoubtedly, the racer's goal was to win; but, he also should have had another goal—to have enough fuel to finish the race. Short-range goals are just as important as long-range goals and a person needs to have *both* working together.

Most of us don't have accomplishments matching our capabilities due to the lack of goal setting. It's not enough to sit idly saying, "I'm just going to sit here until the Lord tells me what to do." He has already told us what to do. It is God's will that we move *toward* a point, toward a *goal*. As Philippians puts it, "I press toward the mark [goal] for the prize of the high calling of God . . ." (3:14).

In essence, we all should be working to accomplish predetermined goals so that if God wants us to reach them, we'll be ready. Then if this goal does not coincide with God's plan for us, He will let us know and change our desires.

In November of 1971, realizing I was among the vast majority who had never stopped to do any goal setting, I determined several goals for myself. One had to do with the war in Indochina. I thought maybe I could contribute in some way by performing on a USO tour in Viet Nam. However, I really knew little about the USO—nevertheless, I told God I was willing. The answer to my prayer came quicker than I could believe because six weeks later I received a telephone call from California asking me to audition for a man taking a group to Viet Nam on a USO "handshake tour." On this kind of tour, the visitors have greater mobility and put heavy emphasis on the one-to-one contact, especially in hospitals, while an "entertainment tour" consists of two one-hour shows a day.

I made it known that the only condition under which I could go would be if I could sing some "message music." With raised eyebrows, he asked what I meant by message music. I explained the message was what the reality of God can do in one's life.

He sort of shook his head *yes* but his voice said, "What?" So I went on to explain that my message music says something of value—not music just for entertainment's sake alone. It's not enough for me to be just an entertainer. There are thousands of entertainers who are good, but to me, it's more important to communicate a message that will increase awareness in the lives of individuals. Anyway, as it turned out, I couldn't go on the trip when he wanted me. Since he really liked what I did, he told me to set my own date and they would organize a tour *around my schedule.* I was thrilled. This was far more than I'd ever imagined—not just going but being able to choose the best, most dedicated performers I could find.

About a month before departure, the USO director flew in to see our show and commented that he was extremely pleased. And he knew we would not disguise our prime motivation for going to Viet Nam—to present the message of God through music.

On arrival, we marvelled at the lush, green beauty of places like Pleiku in the central highlands. I noticed the women staring at me and giggling wherever I'd go. Finally I asked an officer to find out what amused them so much. He returned with the report, "Your height and hair!" They rarely see a woman so tall (I'm five feet seven inches), nor do they often see a woman with true blonde hair, so they all wanted to touch it.

Our show was quite successful. From lively beginning songs we watched the tempo of our foot-tapping, hand-clapping audiences turn to a beautiful, almost reverent quiet of men intently listening as we sang about Jesus Christ.

Our group was of one mind. We knew *why* we were in Viet Nam, *where* every song was leading, and *what* some of the songs had the power to do.

After "Lonely Voices," a haunting song by Billy Hanks, Jr., many of the men openly shared their need for something beyond themselves:

> Lonely voices crying in the city,
> Lonely voices sounding like a child.
> Lonely voices come from busy people,
> Too disturbed to stop a little while.
>
> Lonely faces looking for the sunrise,
> Just to find another busy day.
> Lonely people live in every city,
> Men afraid, but too ashamed to pray.
>
> Lonely eyes I see them in the hallway,
> Burdened by the worries of the day.
> Men at leisure but they're so unhappy,
> Tired of foolish roles they try to play.
>
> Abundant life He came to truly give man,
> But too few His gift of grace receive.
> Lonely people live in every city,
> All they need is only to believe.
>
> Lonely people do I see,
> Lonely voices calling out to me.*

*Copyright © 1967 by Hope Publishing Co. Used by permission.

A few times it was difficult to get through a song when I'd look down on the front row and spot a big, husky soldier looking back with tears in his eyes. It was as though they had been waiting for us.

We didn't speak much throughout the performance because our songs said it all, and we continued to receive comments like the one from a captain at Long Binh. He said he had never come up to a performer before—he never really had a reason to. But he just wanted us to know that this had been one of the most meaningful hours he'd ever experienced in his adult life.

As a result of the message of our show, one helicopter pilot wrote, "There was not a day when I flew a mission that deep down inside I wasn't scared. Now that I know God is with me, I'm not afraid anymore." How many people wish they could say in truth —really deep inside—those last four words: *I'm not afraid anymore.*

As we traveled, we found there was a tremendous boredom factor in Viet Nam, but not in relation to the men who were actively involved in the fighting. In that only 5 percent of the men in Viet Nam were seeing action during the time we were there, the attitudes of those who were engaged in combat were often quite different from those stationed on large bases in relatively safe areas. The servicemen who were flying missions, going out into the bush, and training the Vietnamese civilians to rebuild their country, definitely felt a stronger sense of purpose.

A true parallel to Christian living can be drawn here. Countless spectators go to church but they are not really participants in Christianity. And just like the soldiers in Viet Nam who weren't doing the actual fighting, they get bored. Then a spiritual lethargy sets in that makes it almost impossible for that spectator-Christian ever to "get in the game." Far too many sit on the sidelines and watch, never remotely involved, never considering the possibility of involvement.

I suppose that's why someone I met in Viet Nam was special to me—he was willing to *consider* the possibility of involvement with Christ for himself. The captain of one of the top ten university football teams had just completed a USO handshake tour. The first night, following our 9 P.M. Saigon curfew, the college senior asked me what kind of show we did. I told him about the message music and he said, "I want to talk to you about that later."

Well, we began to talk right then and our discussion, which attracted others, went on for several hours. Suddenly, he excused himself, saying he was going to bed. I was inwardly sorry because I appreciated his honesty and integrity and felt we were getting somewhere. Moments later I left the group and went to my room. To my astonishment, there, waiting for me, was my football player! He quickly explained he didn't want to talk in front of others, so we went at it again.

He told me of someone who had a beautiful type of life that was different from his, but he just couldn't have enough faith to believe. In fact, he said he didn't have *any* faith at all. When I asked if he understood the mechanics of a helicopter engine he answered *no*. "Yet even though you don't understand, you do have enough faith to let choppers carry you all over Viet Nam?" He understood.

I then explained to him God's plan for every man, as clearly as I knew it. Specifically, I shared that believing in Jesus Christ is a matter of three things: the mind, the will, the emotion.

First, the mind. You need to comprehend intellectually who Jesus Christ is, why He came to this earth, and the purpose of His death. Specifically, God saw that man's imperfection would keep him from having the fullest life possible, so the Father sent His Son, Jesus Christ, to live on earth in human form to introduce a *new* way of life. Then at His physical death, Jesus took upon Himself the sin of every person in this world (our past, present, and future sins) so that He could live in the cleansed heart of any man who would ask it.

Second, the will. Either you *will* choose to ask Jesus Christ to take over your life or you *will not* choose to. Once a person is confronted with making this decision there is no middle ground. You can't be *half* alive. Either *you are or you're not,* and no one else can make the decision for you. It must be made on the basis of rational thinking.

Emotion is last. This emotion is not an emotional frenzy or anything fanatical. It's a natural by-product of willfully asking Christ into your life. It's God giving you the ability to love the unlovely. It's God giving you a new heart and when you invite Him into your life, you become a new man inside with new ability to love and to care.

I wound up by explaining to him that there are two types of proof: tangible and experiential. Tangible proof is like seeing a hammer and proving it really exists by picking it up and banging something with it. For experiential proof, you could tell me that such a thing as love exists. But I could say to you, "No, it doesn't. I don't see it. I can't touch it. Does it have a color or sound or scent? Why do you believe in love?"

You would probably tell me, "Because I have experienced it." And you'd be right because you've seen the *effects* of love.

I could look outside and say, "Well, where's the wind? If I can't see it then it doesn't exist." Obviously that's a foolish deduction. I may not be able to see the wind but I have seen *evidences* of the wind rolling the leaves on the ground, waving branches on a tree, tossing a child's kite this way and that, whirling snowflakes up against a house. The effects of the wind I can see, yet invisible to my eyes are the air and the moving forces. Unseen, yes, but quite obviously there.

Consequently, for me to know and feel the wind I must step out into the current; for me to know and feel love, I must step out in faith. For me to know and feel Jesus Christ, *I must step out.*

As we concluded our conversation, my new friend left with a decision yet to be made, but I felt he intellectually comprehended what Christ wanted to do in his life. Later, from the States, he sent me a warm letter telling about some discoveries he

was making. He said he had been reading the Bible and was
really surprised at the depth he was finding. That was something. Reaching out wasn't as painful as he thought it would
be!

Our last day of performance in Viet Nam was especially meaningful to us—it was the Fourth of July. As we flew to another base
the sky was red with fireworks and I really thought it was neat.
Only later did I learn they weren't celebrating the Fourth of July!
Those were tracers—tracers and bullets aimed at us. Fortunately,
their aim was bad and we got down safely.

Following that evening's performance an army major waited to
speak to me. When his turn came, he said with tears in his eyes,
"I'm not a religious man and never have been, but I want you to
know your show really reached me." To me, that one word
reached is the word I brought home. And as we sang to men all
over Viet Nam, I kept praying, "Lord, let the message of this song
reach their hearts."

As I looked at their faces, and into their eyes, I felt they were
reaching to meet us halfway. We threw the possibility of God's
limitless love out to them and they reached for it like hungry
puppies. What an experience!

We closed each performance using "Reach Out And Touch"
as our special message music:

> Reach out and touch a soul that is hungry;
> Reach out and touch a spirit in despair;
> Reach out and touch a life torn and dirty,
> A man who is lonely . . . If you care!
>
> Reach out and touch that neighbor who hates you;
> Reach out and touch that stranger who meets you;
> Reach out and touch the brother who needs you;
> Reach out and let the smile of God touch through you.

Reach out and touch a friend who is weary;
Reach out and touch a seeker unaware;
Reach out and touch, though touching means losing
A part of your own self . . . If you dare!

Reach out and give your love to the loveless;
Reach out and make a home for the homeless,
Reach out and shed God's light in the darkness;
Reach out and let the smile of God touch through you.

11

Witnessing—In My Little Corner of the World

I have a tendency to put God into my private container and say, "God, You can do this and this, but not that. . . ." In truth, I know that God is much bigger than my mind can comprehend. He's not limited to my thoughts about Him even though I still revert to my own little world occasionally. Just as He gives us freedom, we must give Him freedom to move in our lives. He will work through us *if* we permit Him entrance.

An early example of this occurred in my senior year at Hockaday. We had completed a forty-page project on Hamlet and our class was seated in a large circle discussing how tired we were of the play. Just as we all agreed to try to get the teacher off the subject, she walked in and sat down at her desk which was a part of the circle.

"I hate God," blurted out a straight *A* student whose eyes were fixed straight on me from across the room. Then all eyes bounced in my direction. I managed to get a sheepish grin on my face, but I didn't pick up the ball. Then she said, "Let me rephrase that: I don't believe in God."

Now I had been a Christian only a little over a year, so a theologian I was not! Yet when all eyes turned toward me, I gathered that was my cue and asked the lengthy, brilliant question, "Why?"

She stated that the Bible was inconsistent and after about fifteen minutes of my attempts to respond to questions, she said, "You really believe in the Bible, don't you? Well, the Bible says 'An eye for an eye and a tooth for a tooth' (*see* Exodus 21:24), and also it says, 'Turn the other cheek' " (*see* Matthew 5:39).

I had no idea what to say so I licked my lips and took a deep breath, just praying for something halfway intelligent to surface. From out of nowhere I found myself saying aloud, "Jesus was the fulfillment of the Old Testament law and He brought a new way of life to every man." Shock! I couldn't believe I said that! That didn't sound like a sentence I would say and in reality, I didn't even know that answer. Even though I didn't speak from my knowledge or my wordage, it was my voice, so all I could think of was, "Thank You, God."

After about ten more minutes of conversation, there was another question I didn't have the answer for, so again I took a deep breath. But just as I opened my mouth, the teacher broke in with, "Okay, you've been asking June all the questions. I think it's time she has the chance to ask some." What timing! I knew God's timing was perfect but this seemed inconceivable!

My first question was, "Is there *anybody* in this room who believes the same way I do?" One girl raised her hand but didn't say anything. It would have meant a great deal if she had been able to do more than just *acknowledge* her Christianity, and I really wished she had been able to share more than her upraised hand.

Answers such as I gave that day hadn't come to me before, nor have they since, and there was a very obvious presence of another Person in the room. I'll never be convinced otherwise. This clearly was not a case of my *abil*ity, but rather my *avail*ability. If I had to pick one word to be the key, the answer, the solution, to achieving life's maximum, it would be the highly undramatic and unheralded word *availability*. Available to God, that is.

Now I'm going to make a confession: there is a mistake in the above paragraph. While this manuscript was being typeset, I was speaking at Arrowhead Springs, California, on this subject, avail-ability. However, the speaker immediately following me had something different to say. Never mentioning my name, he said the key to achieving life's maximum was *useability*. And he was correct.

Neither does it do me, nor anyone else, any good to be *available*, yet not to be *useable*. I might say to God, "If you want, I am available to be a great architect." The only problem is, I can't draw a straight line—even with a ruler! I have not prepared myself for the field of architecture. Available, yes—useable, no.

Now, I could have corrected my mistake without anyone know-ing, but I feel it's important to let others be part of *our learning* experiences.

Please understand, *availability is still essential*. It is a definite prerequisite for useability. For likewise, an individual can be use-able, yet not available.

Knowing that I should always be available and useable is not the same as practicing it. I tend to lose the awareness of this at times. I remember, while waiting for a flight out of Atlanta, I was using the time available to work on a project that needed comple-tion. A man came up and sat down next to me in the lobby. He introduced himself and mentioned that he had something to do with a television appearance I'd made the previous year.

After a moment I remembered him, but thought, "I just don't have time to talk—I've got to get this work done." After chatting a few moments I said, "You know, I just *love* traveling—I get *more* work done! With my heavy schedule, I'm just grateful I can spend the time working. You don't mind if I continue, do you?"

He said he understood and I felt rather smug at how well I'd handled the situation. I continued to work until they called my flight. When I boarded the plane, the man trailed behind me and asked over my shoulder, "Do you mind if I sit by you if I'm no bother?"

"No, not at all," I said. I lied. We talked briefly until the plane was airborne. "Yes, I just love traveling," I brought up again with the finesse of a bulldozer. "No phones, no meetings, no unexpected interruptions. It's great!" Then I excused myself, opened my briefcase, and began my work. I *began* my work, but couldn't keep my mind on it.

I thought, "Now, Lord, You don't really want me to talk to him! You know what all I've got to do."

After a few more minutes I still couldn't concentrate, so I prayed, "Okay, if there's something I'm supposed to say to him, please make it clear." So I shared with him what Jesus Christ had done in my life.

He was an attentive listener. At the end of the flight, he said, "Now I'm beginning to understand why I'm on *this* flight. You see, my plane from Mississippi to Atlanta was late so I missed my earlier connection. Normally, I would have gone to the bar and started drinking. But this time I walked to the bar, put one foot in, and something made me turn around. When I was walking back I couldn't figure out why I did that. Well, now I know." He confided, "I needed to hear everything you had to say!"

During the weekend my "unwelcomed" traveling companion let me know he'd made a commitment to Jesus Christ, and four months later I received a phone call from him. "June, our whole family life is changed. I'm a new man." I felt warm inside and my prayer time that night was full of gratitude.

I learned a great lesson that day: *God has no allegiance to man-made schedules.* If I want to be inattentive and insensitive to others around me, I shall purpose to remain confined to *my schedule.* Otherwise, I have to be willing to let Him scatter my schedule to the winds. I *must* remain available and useable.

I can think of no one whose life changed more dramatically than did the life of Saul (later called Paul) as he experienced being made available to God.

The Book of Acts reports, "At this time there was a great persecution against the church . . . Saul began ravaging the church, entering house after house, dragging off men and women,

committing them to prison" (*see* Acts 8:1). This educated, promi-
nent Jew was also a much-feared murderer. Then it happened!

Can you imagine what that experience must have been like
starting on the Damascus road—literally blinded for three days,
hearing God call *your* name, receiving a miraculous healing touch,
and eventually, becoming the foremost leader of the Christian
church! It would be hard indeed to find a more dramatic experience than Paul's.

Since Jewish names had a direct correlation to the character of
the person, I feel sure it was no accident that he was called Saul
(the name of Israel's first king) until he became a Christian. Then
his name was changed to Paul, meaning *little*. What a promotion!
His new name would serve as a continual reminder of who the
real King was.

Now Paul could have done what so many new Christians do
today—he could have expounded over and over again on his
conversion alone. If that one episode in his life was *all* Paul
shared, he would not have grown spiritually, nor would his efforts
to work in the lives of people have had much depth. Yet Paul went
on to become the world's first and greatest missionary.

Paul chose to *live* Christianity, and Paul knew that *part of
living is sharing*. Initially, he did tell what had happened to him
on that road, but only to substantiate his new position. What's
more, he called himself "the chiefest of sinners"; perhaps *most
needful* rather than *most dramatically called*.

Everyone's conversion experience is different and unique. Because God is a *personal* God it has to be this way. But those
disciples would not have been impressed—not with Paul, anyway.
But with the God who had converted a Saul into a Paul—*yes!*

Paul sought to join himself to Peter and the others, and he
simply told them what had happened. Few believed him at first.
Paul had a past that clung to him like flypaper. It took the
disciples time to watch and listen further to Paul. Finally, they
did believe him, not by his dramatic repetition of his conversion,
but because of his actions. Paul gained more than his original

sight back—he gained a spiritual *insight* that let him know that God's encounter with him was just the beginning of a new life, and not just the end of this reign of terror against the Christians.

His story was dramatic, but that was not Paul's focal point. He saw his conversion experience for what it was—the first step in an exciting adventure. Paul's entire Christian life was an adventure that *started* on the road to Damascus and *grew* from there. That's the secret—*growing* in Christ.

What kind of adventure can you have if your feet remain glued to the same place? Some people have been Christians for twenty years and all they have to share is their initial meeting with God. Personally, I like the kind of Christian who says, "If you're waiting on me, you're backing up." The conversion experience should be the motivation to *grow*—and *go*.

To live Christianity is to experience and share the reality of Christ in every possible way. It is not enough for us to talk about words like *love* and *peace* and *joy*. *We have to live them.*

Joy is not to be equated with happiness. Happiness which consists of good luck, prosperity, and bliss is based on happenings, but happenings will fluctuate. Christ meant for us to have joy— an *inner* joy which is constant, immovable, and unchanged by circumstances.

I can still see the perplexed look on the face of a beauty salon manager telling me about a Christian woman who had gone through unbelievable adversities. "Bad things keep happening to her, yet she seems so genuinely happy. *Nothing* seems to faze her." Apparently the woman had roots of inner joy (this is part of that "peace that passes all understanding" Christ talks about), and as a result, she was a strong witness making a profound impression on this manager—perhaps without even knowing it.

This word *witness* needs to be understood. Webster's defines it as, "One who beholds, or otherwise has personal knowledge of anything; that which furnishes evidence or proof and 'testimony' "—which means a "declaration made to establish some fact."

Suppose you're walking down the street and a fellow runs out of a jewelry store carrying a bundle. The owner of the store is in hot pursuit, and you're a witness to what happened. Consequently, you could give a testimony to establish some facts; but more importantly, you *could* say something to change the outcome, hopefully for the better. You not only could, but you *should.*

Move the word *witness* over into the Christian life and its meaning doesn't change. When we share with others what God did and does in our lives, we are sharing personal knowledge, evidence, and proof of what happened. Again, what is most important is that the outcome of *another person's life could be changed* for the better.

Some have the misconception that witnessing is always verbal. Not so! Many times it would be highly inadvisable to say anything when being an example—being a silent witness—could say more than a thousand words. In other words, *the timing must be right* to speak.

However, this we can know for sure: God wants us to be *both* kinds of witnesses. He teaches us how to be sensitive to verbal and nonverbal situations. It's a matter of our availability—letting God just move in and take over! Then, as a result, our useability and sensitivity to others increase in proportion.

You've heard about the cobbler whose children had no shoes, the carpenter whose doors hung loosely from their hinges, the insurance salesman who died with no insurance. Those closest seemed to be ignored or uncared for in each case.

A sincere friend in college told me: "I try to *live* Christianity. People can see it so I don't need to talk about it."

I couldn't find agreement with her because it's not good enough just to be good. Many people are good—good for nothing! Their *goodness* stands for *nothing.* Where are the people who are good for *something?*

Living a good life is not all that Christ asks us to do. He said, "Go and tell." This means not only *living* but *sharing* the recipes of your Christian beliefs. When we discover an ingredient that helps us live more effectively, we need to share it. In reality, the person who *really lives* Christianity would have to work extremely hard *not* to talk about it. A natural part of living is sharing. I've watched outstanding individuals who've really challenged me, but I can't follow them around all day with a tape recorder and a movie camera. I need them to *share* with me some important insights which have helped them grow.

Look at Paul's letters. His instructions to growing Christian leaders require them to *act* on their faith.

> *Pray* much for others.
> *Read* and *explain* the Scriptures.
> *Encourage* them to do right.
> Never be afraid to *tell* others about our Lord.
> You must *teach* these things.
> *Speak* up for the right living.
> *Share* your faith with others.

All are ingredients for Christian living. Merely living is not enough—"Go and tell."

One time when I was speaking at a university, I said that any true Christian who refrains from talking about Christ to others because he is shy is actually hiding behind an excuse. The one who says, "I'm a shy person," needs to replace the word *shy* with *selfish.* That individual is saying, "I'm more important than other people. Even if there is a chance that I could help them, I don't know what they might think of me. So I won't say anything."

After the program, a girl with waist-length hair came up to me and said, "I felt like you were talking just to me the whole time. I had no idea I was doing that, but it's so clear now." A month later she let me know that not only had her actions changed, but also her relationships with people had improved tremendously.

But what about those of you who say, "I want to talk to others but I just can't." Well, maybe *you* can't. But God can! In this instance, *availability* really is the key.

As Ian Thomas states in the power-packed *Saving Life of Christ* ". . . all the inexhaustible supplies of God are *available* to the man who is *available* to the inexhaustible supplies of God."

But how do you take that giant step from being *available* to being *useable?* This is an often-asked question.

Recently while I was singing in Ridgecrest, North Carolina, several teen-agers came to me with this problem. They wanted to be better witnesses on their campuses, but, "We just don't know what to say."

In a few moments they all realized that, while they were *willing* to share their faith with others, they simply couldn't—not because they weren't able, but because they were spiritually stale. Sadly enough, they hadn't been feeding on God's food—the Bread of Life, the Bible—therefore, they had nothing nourishing to share.

How can we share if we do not know? Knowledge from God's Word cannot be faked. Many would-be go-and-tellers are just not getting enough to eat. They are starving to death spiritually and it shows in their witness.

The same is true of a child. For many months he depends on someone to feed him and then he begins to feed himself. Finally the big day comes when he learns to feed others.

Unfortunately, some Christians have skipped to the third stage, trying to go through life feeding others, but leaving out the first two stages. They can't understand why they don't have anything of fresh value to share. But how can they share what they haven't got? These potentially great Christians are suffering from spiritual malnutrition—and that's the severest hunger one can know.

12

Meditation—To Succeed or Not to Succeed

Many a man has struggled to make an honest turn from sin in his life. He recognizes the sin for what it is—an enemy to his personal integrity and potential. He seeks to use strategy in order to bridle that which has hold of him, then, with the muscle of his mind and heart, he overpowers his foe to become the conqueror.

However, this man could be heading straight for disaster. If he turns, only to find *nothing* staring him in the face, he will invariably turn back—perhaps to something much worse. It's not enough to *turn from*. One must *turn to*, for when we rid ourselves of something that has been a part of us, a vacancy occurs. But make no mistake—*the void will be filled*. Filled with what? Knowing and understanding *what* can make the difference between being a one-time winner and the ultimate conqueror.

Want to know what *the* weapon is to fight temptation? In Psalms, David says it far better than I: "How shall a young man keep his way pure? By keeping it according to thy Word. . . . Thy Word have I hid in my heart that I might not sin against Thee" (*see* 119:9–11). This is God's solution.

Paul describes the Word of God as "quick, and powerful, and sharper than any two-edged sword, piercing even to the dividing asunder of soul and spirit . . . a discerner of the thoughts and intents of the heart" (Hebrews 4:12).

The Bible has been number one on the world's best-seller list for years. Yet, in most cases it just sits on the shelf as a dust collector. It really makes no difference whether you own one Bible or one thousand, this Book is of little value—until it is *internalized*.

Basically, Christians neglect reading the Bible for two reasons: they can't seem to manage time, and they haven't learned the art of meditation.

How many times have you heard someone say, "I just don't have time to read the Bible!" Actually, the person who makes that statement is precisely correct. Of course we don't have time to read the Bible—not in today's world—we must *make* time.

Let's face it, *you and I always make time for the things we really want to do*. If it's important enough to *us*, it *will* be done. Consequently, we should always *make* time to get deep into God's Word.

I know an investment counselor in his late twenties who, like so many people, was a victim of the late-night television syndrome. He related that at times, "I'd just sit up and watch one program after another until a night was shot." However, realizing that Bible study needed to have top priority in his life, he concluded, "I'll put in the exact number of hours in Bible study as I spend in front of the television set."

Astonished, he later related, "At the end of the first week I found I had twelve hours worth of Bible study to do to even out my TV watching! The hardest part of my project was at the beginning—cutting down on entertaining myself and getting started on some deep study. Yet, the Bible suddenly began to *live* and I was *fascinated!* I couldn't believe that so much I read was relevant to my ordinary secular life. It seemed that God wrote it just to me.

"I guess the old color set misses me. But I don't miss it. I'm just learning too much."

While I don't mean to get on a soapbox about television, I can't resist this column I found in a Presbyterian bulletin:

The Twenty-Third Channel

The TV set is my shepherd. My
spiritual growth shall want.
It maketh me to sit down and do
nothing for His name's sake
because it requireth all my spare
time. It keepeth me from doing my
duty as a Christian because it
presenteth so many good shows
that I must see.

It restoreth my knowledge of the
things of the world, and keepeth
me from the study of God's Word.
It leadeth me in the paths of apathy
and doing nothing in the kingdom
of God.

Yea, though I live to be a hundred,
I shall keep on viewing my TV as
long as it will work, for it is my
closest companion. Its sound and
its picture, they comfort me.

It presenteth entertainment before
me, and keepeth me from doing
important things with my family. It
filleth my head with ideas which differ
from those set forth in the Word of
God.

Surely, no good thing will come of
my life, because my TV leaveth me
so little time to do the will of God.

> Thus I will dwell in the house of
> idleness and sloth forever.

The same concern faced a pro-football player whose wife told me that her husband loved to read the newspaper—every square inch of it! Yet, he gave up his subscription to both Dallas newspapers to spend more time with the Bible. And he didn't stop there. During the Dallas Cowboys' drills, he would review Scripture over and over.

Why did this man feel the necessity for in-depth study of God's Word? Because he had discovered the *food* contained in His Word, and without this food no substantial growth could take place. Feeding on the Scriptures brings us closer to the quality life God promises those who seek Him.

People use up a lot of mileage looking for answers to life's questions—answers that can be found only in the Bible. Some search for truth as though it were to be found glittering in a golden pot at the rainbow's end—always just over the *next* hill. Our God is not a God of fantasy, pretense, or make-believe, and because He knows and accepts our humanity, He knows that even the wisest of the wise shall know only in part.

Christianity is not a plateau where one can sit safely back and say, "Well, I've made it," for our God is a multifaceted God of diversity, creativity, and originality, reaching far beyond the imagination of man's mind. His wisdom and truth are throughout the universe just waiting for explorers such as you and me to discover His hidden treasures—one after another.

God's Word discerns the thoughts and intents of man's heart. How easy it is to fool the people, and sometimes even ourselves. We can learn the language, do the deeds, and wear the righteous robes. However, those who have immersed themselves in God's Word can easily spot a Christian who is not growing.

In college I gave the most inspiring devotional talk on why a person should get into God's Word each day. In fact, it was so good that I was *almost* convinced to do it myself! And occasionally I did try. But something always seemed to happen. I continually skipped over words and verses I didn't understand, or fell asleep while "reading," or just completely forgot to read. But when I did remember, and I came to a verse that spoke to me, I tried to go about it in a very "scholarly" way—like underlining with a red pencil.

Finally my facade had too many holes in it, so after much prayer I decided I would try a project. My entire approach to the Bible had been wrong. When I read it from *my* point of view instead of God's, I found I didn't have much of a view! God sees the whole picture.

It's like a parade. If you have a front-row seat on Main Street while the parade goes marching by, you view only that which is immediately in front of you, but if you get on top of a ten-story building you'll see a lot more. You still won't be able to see the entire parade, however, for while you're watching the front part, the last section is still hidden around the corner. From a helicopter your view would take in the entire parade from start to finish—all at once.

God sees with tremendous accuracy the things needed for our lives. Not only does He see the *past* (the part of the parade that has passed before us which is out of sight) and the *present* (the drums and bugles we see and hear in the *now*), but He also sees the *future* (the part of the parade that is still around the corner). God wants our future to be top quality! Seventy-six trombones and then some!

And it's possible through the Holy Spirit to have this *divine viewpoint* of God as Paul triumphantly proclaims in 1 Corinthians, ". . . we who are spiritual have the very thoughts of Christ!" (*see* 2:16 PHILLIPS).

There are many people who have made me aware of God's principles for successful living. I am especially grateful to Bill Gothard of the Institute in Basic Youth Conflicts who has pointed out that God promises if we do one certain thing we will have success. Let me repeat: God *promises* if we do one certain thing *we will have success!*

The very first message that God inspired David to give in Psalms was, "Blessed is the man . . . his delight is in the law of the Lord; and in his law doth he meditate day and night. And he shall be like a tree planted by the rivers of water, that bringeth forth his fruit in his season; his leaf also shall not wither; and whatsoever he doeth shall prosper" (*see* Psalms 1:1–3). Can you imagine—*anything* we set out to do will be prosperous? But there is a condition: *meditate.* Knowledge comes from man, but wisdom *originates* with God. The two together create a powerful combination which too few possess.

A man is wise when he is able to think God-thoughts, but how can he do that? By understanding that the Bible is the *written Word* of God, thus containing *His* thoughts and *His* wisdom in a multitude of areas. Therefore, the more Scriptures a man absorbs into his mind and heart, the more he will be able to *think God's thoughts!* But the condition: *meditate.*

It took me awhile to get this word *meditate* clear in my thinking. Meditating made it clearer! Someone told me the Book of James was good for a starter. (It sounded good to me because it only had five chapters!) Before beginning I simply prayed, "God, help me get something out of this." Then I took the first chapter and tried to see it from the Lord's viewpoint as though He would be speaking to me directly. After all, the Bible was written by God to believers and since I was a believer, it was written to me! I personalized it—when the pronoun *you* was used, I mentally changed it to *me.*

As Dale Evans Rogers points out, "The Bible, God's Holy Word, is not to be read like any other book, or like a magazine; too many blessings are lost unless it is read as a personal message from God Himself."

When I found verses that were especially applicable to me, I underlined them. Having completed the chapter, I chose one verse to write on an index card and kept repeating it over and over. I then meditated on that verse, thinking on it, applying it to my life, praying, "God, what are You trying to teach me in this verse?"

How quickly I learned that God had many insights to teach me, if only I would let Him, if only I would give Him my time. The next morning before letting my feet touch the floor, I looked at the card again and began to *think* on it. I became astounded at the amount of time I had wasted *reading* the Bible without understanding.

In turn, I discovered there were times in the day ideal for meditation which previously I would have considered unusable: getting ready in the morning, preparing for bed at night, walking between classes, driving in my car—anywhere I could flip out that card and start meditating.

As I progressed in this project, my collection of index cards grew fatter and my verses grew longer. I learned later that one should meditate on whole sections of Scripture (and complete chapters) in order to keep God's Word in context, but the important thing I learned was that as we assimilate the Scriptures consistently and thoroughly, they actually become a part of our thinking and flow from us as easily as if they'd always been there.

The experience I had with a Dallas newcomer proved to be so delightful that I must share it. While I was counseling with this attractive career woman, we determined that meditation was the area in which she was lacking strength. After I shared my project with her, she agreed to try it for seven days, beginning in James and then going into Matthew.

A week from that day at a party, she came running up to me, exclaiming, "It's fantastic! You know, I've never been able to get anything out of the Bible before. I always thought it was so boring, and nobody could have convinced me that I'd ever be excited about what I was going to learn the next day through the Bible. Oh, but June, I hope it's okay—instead of going into Matthew, I went into Collisions, and that's really a cool Book." Bless her. It didn't matter what she called it—Collisions or Colossians—so long as she was seeking, and God was speaking, she was in the right Book.

Meditation does require discipline, and the most effective genuine Christians I know are those who have consistently involved themselves in a personal Bible study. Memorizing verses won't cut it, but *the internalization of God's Word in the heart makes victory possible where defeat was inevitable.* The power of the Scriptures stands available, ready upon call for both rich and poor, both great and small, for God is not a respecter of persons.

The president of Princeton University, the governor of New Jersey, and the twenty-eighth president of the United States had this to say:

> I am sorry for the men who do not read the Bible every day; I wonder why they deprive themselves of the strength and of the pleasure. It is one of the most singular Books in the world for every time you open it, some old text that you have read a score of times suddenly beams with new meaning. There is no other book that yields its meaning so personally, that seems to fit itself so intimately to the very spirit that is seeking guidance.
>
> WOODROW WILSON

The Bible means many things to many people: to some it's mythology; to some it's a book of ethics; to some it's philosophy; to some it's the infallible Word of God. If you read it simply as a book of mythology, you will find interesting reading; if you read it just as a book of ethics, you will discover impeccable moral codes; if you read it merely as philosophy, you will thrill at the "propositional truths." But, if you will read it as the *infallible Word of God* you will experience a life changed—

yours!

13

Our Father—Hallowed or Hollow Be Thy Name

Over the last few years, God's holiness has been a constant wonder and mystery to me. Unfortunately, too many take lightly the name of God and the very Personage of God Himself.

First and foremost, God is a *holy* God. I say again, GOD IS A HOLY GOD. But I fear even the church has lost the awareness of this despite 1 Thessalonians 4:8, which declares, "It is not for nothing that the Spirit God gives us is called the *Holy* Spirit" (PHILLIPS).

So holy is He that for thousands of years people revered God with such awe they would not even speak His name. The Hebrew word for their God was Yahweh, but it could only be uttered by the high priest and then only once a year. This complete reverence for the divine name is foreign to many today who flippantly refer to God as The Man Upstairs, Big Daddy in the Sky, and other such terms. If they only knew!

In talking with Eugenia Price about the holiness of God she said, "I've written many books about God, but what boggles me most is that a God so holy can be my Friend, too."

I replied, "When I think of God's holiness I am staggered—my mind simply cannot comprehend God." I stammered in my attempt to say something really concrete about this subject and finally added, "I just don't know how to express His holiness."

We need to return to the biblical concept of God. Yes, He is our Friend. Yes, He is our Comforter and our Saviour. Yes, He is our Father. But above all else, He is our God! We need to sing more often and with more awe, "Holy, Holy, Holy, Lord God Almighty!"

In the light of God's holiness I am convinced there is no place in the Christian life for mediocrity. God never calls us to a task, only to leave us floundering in the middle of it. Someone once said, "If you feel far away from God, guess who moved?"

God demands holiness because it is *His* reputation that is at stake in the lives of those who call themselves Christians. This is precisely why a mediocre Milquetoast Christian is such an affront to the holiness of God. Anyone who bears the name Christian, but who is so tepid that he can flow into the world unnoticed and mix with the world without causing a change of temperature, is an abomination to God. He states it plainly in Revelation, "Would that you were cold or hot! So, because you are lukewarm, and neither cold nor hot, I will spew you out of my mouth!" (3:16 RSV).

God is very definite about man's attempt to keep one foot in the Word and the other in the world. With Him there is no lukewarm, no middle ground, no rationalization, no compromise. How many have taken the name Christian (Christ-in-one) only to fail to live up to its implication, and thus, let it fall to the ground. Either carry the name of Christ in honor, letting His power take the control, or claim no association with His name at all.

I realize that "conformity" is an unpopular principle. The new morality says, "Drop the yoke of Puritanical guilt. No one has the right to dictate morality! Nothing is wrong as long as it doesn't hurt anybody." An example is Ernest Hemingway's famous definition: ". . . what is moral is what you feel good after and what is immoral is what you feel bad after."

But anyone who has a flippant disregard for the code of ethics outlined in the Bible fails to perceive the holiness of God for to *know* him is to *obey* Him.

As Paul pleads with the Christians ". . . let us cleanse ourselves from all filthiness of the flesh and spirit, perfecting holiness in the fear of God" (2 Corinthians 7:1).

When one truly perceives the holiness of God, he not only begins to reflect the image of Christ, but also reacts in submission to God's will. When Isaiah saw a manifestation of God's holiness in the temple, he reacted with humble obedience. "Here am I, send me" (*see* Isaiah 6:8).

God seeks only men who will purpose to follow His leadership —*no matter the cost.*

I cannot imagine Jesus Christ instructing Peter and the other disciples, "Okay, fellows, you go ahead of me into Bethany, and start a pep rally in the town square. Begin with a low chant of my name and progressively get louder until the crowd is large, excited, and the sound is deafening. Get everyone yelling, "J-E-S-U-S"— then I'll come in and give my speech."

In rereading the words I have just written I cringe because this is so foreign to what the Bible tells us of Jesus' ministry. He was the Prince of Peace and the above supposition suggests anything but a calming aura. He is not caught up in Jesus cheers or "Rev- 'em up" techniques. *God does not need man-made gimmicks.* If only man could be convinced of that.

Please do not misunderstand. There is no substitute for genuine enthusiasm. Enthusiasm is one of the necessary, obvious signs of a Christian who has got it all together. Enthusiasm on its own is contagious, but in a frenzied enthusiasm one loses sight of the awesome, all-powerful God.

But the Lord never uses manufactured enthusiasm to achieve His results. Unfortunately, many have turned upside down the order in which God works, not realizing that enthusiasm is a *natural by-product* of personal spiritual growth.

I've observed that those who are constantly in the Word of God continually *draw people* to Christ with lasting results because they're not based on emotionalism.

Contrary to emotionalism is faith; faith not based on feeling, because faith is based on *fact—the fact of the Word of God.*

Whatever our degree of reverence and obedience to God, it seems pitifully small when I think of Abraham's response to one of God's commands.

God spoke to Abraham and told him to take his son, Isaac, and offer him as a burnt offering. Genesis 22 gives no indication that Abraham questioned God in any way. It very simply states that Abraham rose up early the next morning, took his beloved son, and headed for the place of sacrifice God was to reveal to him.

When father and son reached their destination, Abraham set about to bind his son, place him on an altar, and lay wood about the boy. As Abraham took his knife from its sheath and was about to slay his son, God intervened: "Lay down the knife; don't hurt the lad in any way for I know that God is first in your life—you have not withheld your beloved son from me" (*see* v. 12 LB).

God was testing Abraham and he passed the most difficult test anyone could encounter—that of unwavering obedience.

Now we can't appreciate the full impact of Abraham's obedience unless we present this same request to John Doe—twentieth century:

"You want me to do what? Sacrifice my son? Absolutely not! It's not in our contract. . . . Be reasonable. You promise an "old man" a boy, then you want him for a sacrifice. There's no logic in that! . . . Look, let me check with my attorney . . . okay? I think we can work out a compromise. Money is no object. . . . Wait! I've got it. I'll have Isaac call in my staff of engineers and we'll design a boat that will make Noah's look like a canoe! . . . Look. I know I haven't been that committed—but all that's going to change. I'll head all those committees—catch up on my tithes— buy another church bus. . . . Let's face it: I'm desperate! If there is *one possible alternative*, give it to me—anything!"

Sounds foolish, doesn't it? But Abraham didn't question God one whit. He set out immediately to do what God asked of him. His God was holy and if there was a "why?" in Abraham's mind (and there must have been) he never expressed it. He was too busy *doing* what God asked to *dwell* on queries.

Again, I think of that Scripture in 1 Samuel: "Speak, Lord; for thy servant heareth" (*see* 3:9).

How many times has the eternal "Why?" been asked with regard to painful circumstances in our lives? Every man has experienced the feeling of being pulled apart—pulled by the force of circumstances he cannot control in a world he did not make.

"Why?" It's all right to *ask* the question but it's wrong to *demand* the answer. Nothing happens *to the believer* by mistake. ". . . all things work together for good to them that love God" (Romans 8:28).

One cannot fathom the many possible ways the Lord uses tragedies to benefit those within and without the family circle. He can even affect lives of people unknown to the individuals suffering.

Let me share an incident which few know of concerning the former minister of music who served the First Baptist Church in Dallas for fourteen years. This vibrant man, whose dedication influenced thousands, not only through his beautiful singing, but also through his *life*, was leading the music in a small town when he was taken ill and went into a coma.

When the news came about Lee Roy Till, my mother flew in my father's company plane to take his wife and children to him, and then later that evening to bring him and his family back to Baylor Hospital in Dallas.

The same afternoon Mother left, I was due to go to Louisiana to sing at a youth rally. In order for me to fit the rally into my schedule, I had arranged to charter this same plane weeks before.

When I got to the airport, I didn't see the plane. Upon inquiring, I learned of the tragedy and that Mother had chartered another plane for me. On arrival at my destination, the pilot of the new charter said he'd like to come hear the program. I was pleased, and that night, much to his surprise and mine, this pilot asked Christ to come into his life. He said that never before had he really understood what Christianity was all about.

Upon returning to Dallas I rushed to the hospital to be with the Tills. In my conversation I mentioned that because of the mix-up in planes something unusual had happened. All in all, it appeared that had it not been for Mr. Till's sudden illness, that pilot would neither have met Jesus Christ that day, nor would he have been confronted with the decision to accept Him that day.

Mrs. Till's response reflected a depth in God which was beautiful: "Well, if one soul could be saved through this tragedy then it's worth it. My husband would be the first to agree." God's specialty is *redeeming* tragedy because God Himself is the Redeemer.

How well David had learned this lesson as he declared, "It is good for me that I have been afflicted; *that I might learn thy statutes*" (Psalms 119:71 italics added).

I do not question that in the heart of those suffering the pain and the hurt, the sorrow still is very real and very present. However, such assurance washes away the paralyzing fears and moments of meaninglessness: "They that sow in tears shall reap in joy" (Psalms 126:5).

14

Temptation—A Familiar Face

My father had always advocated foods that are healthy for the body. To him that meant little seasoning, no candy, nor things made with white sugar or white flour. (Well, that eliminated everything that tasted good!) All these were on the enemies-to-the-body list.

This food plan didn't go over too well with his offspring. Being typical children, we loved sweets and would hide cupcakes, candy bars, and other goodies, either in the basement or in a bottom drawer in the kitchen where we knew Dad wouldn't look.

After school, we'd raid our hidden treasure chest, retreat to the TV room, and devour our palatable pleasures. By dinner I was never too hungry and can recall eating the meat, and the vegetables if I liked them. But we *did* have desserts.

My father believed the heart of the apricot seed to be so nutritious and healthful that we ate apricots at every meal just to get the seeds. We had apricot whips and apricot toppings, stewed apricots, just plain apricots, apricot cobbler, apricot jam and jelly, apricot cake—any and all forms of apricots.

I remember not long after our two-year stint with apricots, I came home to find an unopened pastry box on the kitchen table. I opened the box only to discover a familiar face. You guessed it —an apricot pie! Even though pie is my favorite dessert, I could not go another apricot in *any* form. Thus, I did not yield to the temptation to eat it because, simply put, it was no temptation.

But how would I have reacted if it had been a definite temptation for me: What if coconut cream pie had been the delicacy instead of something that didn't appeal to me?

Many times we take credit for resisting a temptation when in reality we're just refusing something we don't enjoy. I could piously say, "I *never* eat llama stew!" For one thing, I've never had the opportunity (which is probably my good fortune), and, too, llama stew doesn't exactly sound appetizing.

What about these situations which are real temptations to us? I have learned that we should determine what course of action to follow *before* temptation strikes; then, when tempted, the decision has already been made. Proverbs says: "A prudent man foresees the difficulties ahead and prepares for them; the simpleton goes blindly on and suffers the consequences" (22:3 LB).

An example of this happened to me recently. Because my schedule had been so full, I knew I had to stay up all night working on some material for a retreat. In the early hours of the morning I finished, but I knew I had to sit down right then and reread what I'd written because there was no other time. My plane was scheduled to leave early and I hadn't packed yet. Rather than choose to sit in a straight-back chair, I thought I'd just prop myself up in bed and read. That way I could at least rest my body.

I should have realized that as tired as I was, in order to accomplish anything, I would have to stay clear of any piece of furniture that put me in a horizontal position. At that point, it didn't even have to be soft! I awoke a few hours later, with just enough time to throw my things in a suitcase and hurry to catch my plane.

A situation can be either a temptation or a test—a *temptation* to yield or a *test* to strength, and *we* determine which it will be. For example, there are times (very few, I must admit) when I am dieting that I can look at a piece of pie and not find it tempting —it becomes a test. You see, I have *already made up my mind not to yield.* I have predetermined my course of action. But if I were to sit and dwell on thoughts of the pie, it would become a temptation. I would have permitted that pie to become so attractive that before long I would find it too difficult not to give in, and in the end I *would have been the cause for my own downfall.* This same principle is true of any temptation, however large or small, and whatever the extent of its effect on our lives.

Some situations which aren't a matter of right or wrong can prove to be hindrances. For instance, when I jog it might look strange if I tied a bowling ball to my leg and strapped a television to my back. Would people consider it a sin to do that? No, but those things would obviously slow me down. (I'm being optimistic —I couldn't run two steps!) That's what many things do in our lives. They slow us down and keep us from operating at our maximum.

Sin is not limited to the Ten Commandments—sin is *anything* outside of His perfect plan for our lives. It just may be that there are a number of things in our lives which God considers sin about which we've never given a second thought. God says to us: Let go of those hindrances and run free!

Temptation wears more masks than New Orleans at Mardi Gras and we're all duping ourselves when we fail to admit that one of our greatest temptations is the misuse of time. I would like to say with Bernard Berenson, "I wish I could stand on a busy street corner, hat in hand, and beg people to throw me all their wasted hours."

Let's suppose that each morning your bank credited your account with $1,440, under one condition: Whatever part you fail to use during the day would be erased from your account—no balance to be carried over. What would you do?

You'd draw out every cent every day and use it. Well, we do have such a bank, and its name is *time*. Every morning it credits you with 1,440 minutes. It rules off as forever lost whatever portion you have failed to invest to a good purpose, nor is there any drawing against tomorrow.

How can one use time to his best advantage? By carefully using the most marvelous and unique part of man—his mind. Our brains are like computers—they store every bit of information fed into them with the possibility of recall at any time, wanted or unwanted.

Now this is the concern: God says, "As a man *thinketh* in his heart, so is he" (*see* Proverbs 23:7). If some of the information stored in a man's "computer" is less than desirable, he has a problem, because *the starting point of sin is in the mind.* Repeated sinful *thought* results in sinful *action,* and repeated sinful action results in sinful *habits.*

This is precisely why God says to meditate day and night. Inundating the mind with Scriptures will help counteract the negative information breeding in our storage chambers. The choice is ours—we can either reinforce the *cause* of sin or reinforce the *cure.*

Not long ago I thought I'd take the evening off to go to a movie, but when I turned to the newspaper's amusement section I found only two shows which weren't rated *R* or *X.* What a choice! I stayed home.

God's rating system is in Proverbs: "A wise man is hungry for truth, while the mocker feeds on trash" (15:14 LB).

The whole point is—*What's the point?* I see no value in recycling trash (in our minds) if the end product is trash. One never needs to *experience* sin in order to *know* sin.

Obviously our rating system has definite inaccuracies. That's why I would prefer to go by what Paul advises in Philippians: "Whatever is true, honorable, right, pure, lovely, of good repute, let your mind dwell on these things" (*see* 4:8).

My answer to why we should avoid anything the least bit questionable lies in 1 Corinthians 10:31: ". . . whatever you do, do all to the glory of God" (RSV).

We cannot bring any glory to God or any benefit to our minds by subjecting ourselves to anything that will tempt us to focus our attention on unclean thoughts and desires.

Carl Gustav Jung stated, "The central wrong of our time is emptiness." If true, can that emptiness be filled wisely with such things as lurid sensuality or bloody violence? We read in Proverbs 6:27, "Can a man hold fire against his chest and not be burned?" (LB).

Fortunate for us, His Word says, "No temptation has overtaken you but such as is common to men; and GOD IS

FAITHFUL, who will *not allow you to be tempted beyond what you are able;* but with the temptation will provide the way of escape also, that you may be able to endure it" (*see* 1 Corinthians 10:13).

In other words, the largest as well as the smallest temptation in our lives God will conquer—*if* we will let Him, and that's a promise!

Somehow, everything goes right back to the cross. Through Christ's death He overcame sin, and likewise, He has given us the *power to overcome* all temptation and sin.

While leading a retreat, I saw many attitudes change with regard to temptation. I had asked some boys to make a six-foot wooden cross and plant it in the ground. Silhouetted against the sky at dusk, it was a very impressive focal point for the young people sitting around it.

Everyone was given a pencil and a piece of red paper, and asked to write down one specific sin which he or she had recently committed—not a big general sin like, "I don't love my fellow man as I should," but something very explicit. I also told them no one would see their papers—what they wrote was personal—just between them and God.

After they had finished, I told them to go and nail the paper on the cross. One by one each slowly nailed his sin to the cross while we sang, "Were You There When They Crucified My Lord?" When all had returned, they saw that their sins had covered the cross—the natural wood was covered with red!

Just as the blood of an unspotted lamb acted as a covering for the sins of God's chosen people, the Jews, so also did the blood of Christ act to blanket our sins so that we could know freedom —freedom from all sin.

Jesus died for our sins so that we might experience true life, not mere existence. But His death is meaningless unless we *claim* His victory. There is no burden too big, no temptation too tall, no sin too sordid.

If we have nailed a sin to the cross, do we really want it back? Why not leave it there! After all *Jesus did die for it.*

15

Forgiveness—To the Very End

For years Mother thought she was very clever, because after our naps (if we'd been good), she would reward us with raisins which are rich in iron and vitamins. I thought that was a treat until I found out how tempting candy was.

Once when Mother and I were in a drugstore, I spied the candy bars stacked neatly on the eye-level shelf and my mouth began to water. When no one was looking, I slid a Three Musketeers candy bar into my hand and slipped outside the drugstore. I'll never forget that moment! I shoved that whole candy bar into my mouth so fast I could hardly chew. I assumed that if I asked Mom to buy me some candy, she wouldn't.

After Mother had finished her shopping, we got into the car and headed home. Suddenly she looked at me and asked, "What is that chocolate doing all over your face?"

I quickly pulled the innocent bit, "Chocolate? What chocolate?" But there was no way to hide the fact—I'd been found out. She saw the facts smeared all over my cheeks!

Out came the switch, but the hard part was that Mother made me go back to give a nickel to the store manager and ask him to forgive me. The whole ordeal was extremely humiliating. I remember thinking: Isn't it enough that I got a spanking? No, it wasn't. And later I was to learn more about asking forgiveness.

Meanwhile, Mother used a most effective method of discipline where it seemed I did most of the work. If I did something wrong, she would confront me with the situation and ask me a few questions to lead me to admit I had done wrong. Then she would ask *me* to go outside and pick a limb off the tree for the spanking. If I got a branch that was too small, she would get a whopper.

After I brought in the switch, she would tell me to go up to my room and wait. Then after trimming a little "extra" off the limb, she would eventually come upstairs and ask me to bend over the bed. Then she would lay the limb on my limbs pretty hard. At the time I wouldn't have thought too highly of Proverbs, "A youngster's heart is filled with rebellion, but punishment will drive it out of him" (22:15 LB).

By the time Mother got through I didn't think I had any rebellion left—or hide, either. I'm grateful for my mother's way of correcting me. I knew I had done wrong and was troubled with a sense of guilt. Mom's method had a threefold effect: it gave us a chance to come to grips with my guilt, together; I felt she shared this problem with me. It provided a punishment I could understand—one comparable to the crime; and it established a definite time and place for me to be rid of it *once* and for *all*.

Mom never punished me with anger. She was always composed (which I certainly was not) and she would say, "I am doing this because I love you and one day you will understand." At these times and as a result of her spirit, I always understood that she disapproved of my *action* rather than *me*.

Now, from my experience of working with hundreds of parents, I especially realize the value of her being consistent—even when it wasn't convenient! Many parents will not stop their work or even interrupt a telephone conversation when their child needs correcting. Their neglect leaves the child with inner frustration. Unfortunately, they will both pay for it later; for a child who is permitted to get away with acts he knows are wrong will attempt worse things later. In other words, *it is easy to dodge responsibilities, but we cannot dodge the consequences of dodging our responsibilities.*

Just as parents have responsibilities to their children, the reverse is definitely true. Most children, including teen-agers, *expect* to have food on the table, *expect* to have a roof over their heads, *expect* to have clothes to wear.

Apparently, young people don't realize the role in which God has placed them and what their response is to be toward their parents. In truth, there is no greater joy a parent can experience than to have a genuinely *grateful* child. Shakespeare said it very well: "How sharper than a serpent's tooth it is to have a thankless child."

One day I realized that I, too, had been a part of the silent majority. For years I had never said one *thank you* for the things my father had provided me. I decided to talk to Dad one evening. He was sitting in the dining room when I walked in and, for once, there were not a lot of people around. "Dad, may I talk to you a minute?" I asked.

Never taking his eyes off the evening paper, he answered yes. Then I began simply to thank him for all he had done for me and I asked if he would forgive me for taking him for granted. He paused, looked up over his reading glasses which were perched down on his nose, and responded with a broad smile, "That's all right, June. The pleasure was all mine." How I wish I had shown him my gratitude long before. I should have, but I didn't.

God puts a high priority on our relationships with people—all people. In fact, in Matthew, He says if you're giving an offering at the altar and you remember a friend has something against you, leave your offering and make it right with your friend—*then* return to give your offering.

"Pride ends in destruction; humility ends in honor" (Proverbs 18:12 LB). The most dangerous prayer one can pray is, "Forgive us our trespasses as we forgive those who trespass against us." In other words, "Lord, deal with me in the same manner as I deal with those who offend me." The natural man bases his forgiveness of others on their worthiness, or their promise not to do it again, or their attitude, or how much they have offended him.

However, this God of complete power and control knows only

unconditional forgiveness. His heart holds no strings, His love lists no limits.

There is not a soul alive who has not wronged another person and in turn needed forgiveness from that person. So what do we make of the one unwilling to forgive another? Doesn't refusing to forgive suggest he is trying to put himself *above* God?

I'm afraid the answer to this question may be yes. I have three reasons to substantiate this statement. First, there is nothing for which *God* is not ready to forgive us if we would but ask. Second, putting the offense of a man *above* the person, himself, shows complete disregard for the value God places on each individual. And last, there is one Scripture which cannot be erased from the Bible nor rationalized away by our stubbornness! "Vengeance is *mine;* I will repay, saith the Lord" (Romans 12:19 italics added). This suggests it is *God*—not man—who has the final word. And how dramatically this is illustrated in the life of Joseph.

Has there ever been a man in history who ever accomplished any more, politically, than Joseph? He was sold to the Ishmaelites by his jealous brothers, carted off to a foreign country, imprisoned for a crime he didn't commit, but eventually became ruler of Egypt—second only to Pharaoh.

For years his father had been told his favorite son was dead— a victim of a wild beast. And just when it seemed that Joseph was a victim of circumstances, God initiated a stupendous turn of events. Because of a seven-year famine, Joseph's brothers were told by their father, Jacob, to go to Egypt and buy grain. As Joseph was governor of all Egypt, he was in charge of the sale of grain; therefore, it was to him his brothers had to come. Joseph, recognizing his brothers, gave orders for each one's sack to be filled with as much grain as he could carry, and also to put into the sacks the money each had paid for the grain. It appeared that the brothers were stealing—what an opportunity to even the score!

But Joseph scorned this opportunity for vengeance. The second time the brothers returned, he said with tender emotion, "I am

Joseph, your brother, whom you sold into Egypt." He went on to tell them not to be angry with *themselves* because of what they had done. *"God did it! He sent me here ahead of you to save your lives. God sent me here, not you."* And he added, "I will take care of you."

I believe this is a classic example of *total forgiveness!* Joseph was in a perfect position to lash out at his brothers. Instead of bitterness he showed only love.

Bitterness and a forgiving spirit cannot live in the same body. Joseph never permitted the two to war within him. He never allowed bitterness the chance to take root.

Do you honestly think that if Joseph had permitted this he would have progressed from a slave to a personal servant to an overseer in the house of the captain of the bodyguards? And then from being jailed under false charges, would have progressed to prison supervisor and then to ruler of Egypt?

Joseph would never have made it, because when one is embittered against another, he is permitting that other person to control him emotionally. Bitterness has a way of burrowing deep inside us, not allowing freedom. Emotional control by another person is a constrictor and can stifle us physically, emotionally, and spiritually. Bitterness is clearly the result of lack of forgiveness.

But Joseph was both *freed* and *free* because he had placed his life in God's hands. And where God lives, bitterness flees. His brothers stood in amazement as he assured them, "I will take care of you." A beautiful result of someone letting God *be* God in his life!

We're quick to think, "I would have forgiven them, too." We feel we do have forgiving spirits, but do we really comprehend what Jesus deems fundamental in forgiveness?

Peter didn't. He wanted to know, ". . . how many times can my brother wrong me and I must forgive him? Would seven times be enough?" (Matthew 18:21 PHILLIPS).

"No," replied Jesus, "not seven times, but seventy times

seven!" (v.22). What a challenge! Forgiveness means *everybody, everything, every time.*

Unconditional forgiveness in its purest sense is the essence of God.

Jesus was near two men who certainly had no peace within them. Hanging on crosses on both sides of Him were two thieves suffering the agonies of crucifixion and most likely letting their pain be heard.

A look at the thieves shows that despite the fact that the situation seemed hopeless, many thoughts crossed their tired, tortured minds. No man sentenced to death ever gives up hope for a life-saving intervention.

Yet, never had they considered that help was hanging right next to them. The Man in the middle was to free one of the thieves from his cross. The Man in the middle. That is exactly who Jesus is today—the Mediator between us and God.

But to the thieves, Jesus was just another piece of humanity as near death as they. Perhaps one thief had noticed that Jesus' suffering was quiet. When Christ did open His mouth, it was to utter a sentence. One very short sentence got through to this thief, and he couldn't believe what he heard.

"Forgive them" (*see* Luke 23:34).

Out of the corner of his eye, the thief caught a glimpse of the face of the Man in the middle. He saw anguish and pain and torment, far beyond what had been inflicted upon himself, and what he saw made him wonder how this Man was still alive. Yet, through Jesus' obvious suffering, he witnessed a mystical peace and tranquility which confounded him. This was beyond his comprehension and caused him to acknowledge who Jesus was. And so, Luke records the thief addressing Jesus as *Lord* and saying, "Lord, remember me when thou comest into thy kingdom" (*see* Luke 23:42).

Acknowledging Jesus as Lord is the opening of that door to His Kingdom, and our Lord was quick to respond with, "Today shalt thou be with me in paradise" (*see* v.43).

Before His death the Lord's last earthly act was to redeem a soul! He came into the world for this purpose and left the world carrying out this purpose to the very end.

For this thief, God's timing was perfect. But what was the other thief thinking? Did he hear the centurion say, "Truly this man was the Son of God" (Mark 15:39)?

Once there were three and now there was one. This remaining one could find no solace in saying, "I died next to the Son of God!"

God is the God of the second chance and for this thief, his second chance was never used. He died.

How close he was, yet how far away.

16

Decision—With Gratitude

"All that I know about me I give to all that I know about You."

This was the simple, childlike prayer of a young girl asking Christ into her life. The beauty of it is more than touching.

"Lord, I realize I have not lived a perfect life. I know I have sinned. But, I want Your best in my life so I ask You to forgive me for the many times I've failed and to make me the total person You created me to be. Thank You for hearing and acting on my prayer."

These words came from an adult. Yet somewhere between these two prayers is what I said when I asked Christ into my life at age fifteen. But whether your prayer is one sentence or a lengthy outpouring, God hears and does *act* upon any request for admittance into your heart.

Salvation is a gift. ". . . the gift of God is eternal life through Jesus Christ" (*see* Romans 6:23).

At a wedding reception in another town, a woman said, "June, I want you to have this gift. I'm just going to put it on this credenza and you can get it when you leave." I thanked her for the gift; however, much later I realized I had forgotten and had left the present.

Now, was that gift really mine? Even though it was given to me freely, it's not mine until I take it. We "take" salvation by simply asking for it—personalizing it—receiving that which was *already* given.

Before I asked Christ into my life, it always bothered me when someone would ask me if I were a Christian. I would quickly think: Well, yes, isn't it obvious? I go to a Christian church. Then I realized that just because I walk inside a church, that doesn't make me a Christian. Internalizing Jesus Christ in my life does.

Let me illustrate. In order to derive any value from food, it must be taken internally. The miracle of food cannot be experienced until we internalize it—only then can it rebuild damaged tissues; only then can food give us the energy which we (on our own) cannot produce. Food sustains us physically just as Christ sustains us spiritually. Yet often we keep Him on the outside, while all along He wants to come within to give us power which we do not have, and to rebuild the damaged areas of our lives.

How can we know Christ is *inside?* Revelation 3:20 tells us that He can stand outside the door of our hearts and knock and knock and knock, and we can hear His voice, but until we open our hearts to Him and invite Him in, nothing happens; thus Jesus Christ is not a part of our lives. I love that picture of Jesus standing outside and knocking. If we have sincerely asked Jesus Christ into our lives, He promises to enter in order to become the Lord of our lives.

Perhaps you say, "Well, sometimes I have doubts." If you know there has been a time when you've truly asked Jesus Christ to take over the controls of your life, yet you still have doubts, continue to repeat the assurance that God gives us: "I will never leave you nor forsake you" (*see* Hebrews 13:5). It is a promise from God, and God's promises are the surest of all promises.

Prior to my personal confrontation with Jesus Christ, God had always been to me a church—not a choice; a devotional tidbit—not a full-course feast on His Word; an obligation—not a loving privilege to serve the One who died for me; a religion—not a relationship.

C. S. Lewis, in his book *Miracles: A Preliminary Study*, quotes Thomas Erskin: "Those who make religion their God will not have God for their religion."

Christianity is not my God. God *is* my God! And I have a relationship with Him.

There is a vast difference between having a religion and having a relationship. I could choose from any number of religions in the world, take hold of one, and proclaim loudly, "I've got a religion!" That alone merely implies I have aligned myself with a named organization. I may attend all its meetings, be a very involved, active member, and yet have no affinity except with others in the group. However, Christianity offers a *relationship*—a relationship with God—and because of its very personal nature, lives are changed—made completely new.

A relationship is a revealing of one to another, a closeness in spirit, a personal communication which does not remain static. It changes and grows, for as both parties join together they are able to benefit from each other.

The definition of a relationship is *the state of being related;* therefore, as a person opens his heart to God, he enters into the family of God and becomes a child of the King. We are actually blood related because this miracle of receiving God's best was made possible by the blood of Jesus Christ.

That is why, when someone says to me, "I am a religious person," I can become concerned if no mention is made of a relationship. For that relationship with God is what makes a man a Christian.

Consider this. If you are not experiencing an abundant life, it is not God's fault. This abundant life of which He speaks comes from time spent in His Word. The decision to delve deeply into the Bible is our decision. Neglecting His Word is the result of a decision. Not to decide positively is to decide negatively.

You know, when Christ comes into your life and you really die to self, it's like a hand moving in a glove. You are the glove and Christ is the hand moving. He is the power but you still have your own identity and individuality. It is exciting to know that God's power can be transmitted to us.

One day after a little old lady gave my car a smashing accordion-pleated design, the car dealer handed me the keys to my new automobile. Imagine his surprise if I had placed the keys in the ignition and gone around to the back and pushed the car all the way home, laboring and perspiring over the task. Just as pushing that car would get me nowhere slowly, so do we, as Christians, get nowhere if we rely on our own strength.

The power is within the Christian if he will just call upon Jesus Christ, because He is *all power*. It's not that His way is better, as we sometimes hear. In reality, it's that His way is the *only* way.

When I think of the abundance of God, I think of Jesus' first miracle performed in Cana.

Actually, it must have been a very embarrassing situation for the host for the wine supply ran out in the middle of the festivities. Since water was impure at that time, it would be like having a dinner party today and running out of beverages for the guests.

But Jesus was at the party and He instructed the servants to bring Him six stone water pots filled to the brim with water. The Bible doesn't say how Jesus performed this miracle, but when this new beverage, the converted water, was served to the master of ceremonies, he exclaimed, "This is wonderful." And to the host, "You are different from most. Usually a host serves the best first, and afterwards, when everyone is full and doesn't care, then he brings out the lesser quality. But you have kept the best for the last" (*see* John 2:10 LB).

It was ordinary, clear water that the servants had poured into the pots, but Jesus performed His miracle and gave the water life! The clear impure liquid took on color, taste, dimension, and a beautiful richness.

The man bragging on his host did not know this was all the product of Jesus' touch. It was the best he had ever tasted because Jesus had made it the best! From colorless water, richness emerged. From a colorless life, rich, abundant life can emerge, also. Jesus is the Giver of new life and it comes in the form of the miracle of salvation.

This was His first miracle, but, as with His own life, He saved the best for last. After a drab, lifeless tomb, there followed the Resurrection. That's when abundant life began for all of us.

I was asked one time by my brother-in-law, Randy, if I would call a girl he knew in Dallas, whom he described as "sharp and with it." He felt she needed encouragement, so I telephoned Joanne Altorfer and asked her to come to a program I was doing, and told her we could, perhaps, talk afterwards. She came and at the end of the program opened her life to Jesus Christ for Him to use her in any way.

I saw her a year later and she shared this with me. "June, when you first telephoned, I really didn't want to meet with you. I went to see you only because of my friendship with Randy.

"And I'll tell you something—I thought I knew what *life* was all about, but I found I wasn't even *living.*"

I remember someone saying that I was one of the richest girls in the world. I would have to agree, but I am thinking in terms that are different from theirs.

I am rich first of all because I belong to God. No amount of money in the world could have bought that for me. It was a gift and I chose to accept it.

Next, I am rich in having learned invaluable lessons from both my mother and my father that will remain with me throughout my lifetime.

Finally, I am rich because I have the privilege of sharing my love for Christ with others. Whether it is speaking or singing, it is all sharing the recipe of God's plan for each of us . . . above all else, letting God be God in our lives.

So, rather than THE END, I conclude with living words which know no end:

The grass withers, the flower fades; but the word of our God will stand for ever.

Isaiah 40:8 RSV

THE BEGINNING